D.H. LAWRENCE AND PSYCHOANALYSIS

The Moral Dimension

D.H. LAWRENCE AND PSYCHOANALYSIS

The Moral Dimension

Dr. Vandana Rajoriya
Lecturer in English, GPCK, Sagar, M.P.

ADHYAYAN
ADHYAYAN PUBLISHERS & DISTRIBUTORS
NEW DELHI (INDIA)

Published by
ADHYAYAN PUBLISHERS & DISTRIBUTORS
4378/4B, 105, J.M.D. House, Murari Lal Street
Ansari Road, Darya Ganj, New Delhi - 110002
Ph.: 011-23263018, 011-23277156, Fax: 011-23280028
Email: adhyayanpublishers@yahoo.com

D.H. LAWRENCE AND PSYCHOANALYSIS The Moral Dimension

Edition 2011
ISBN 978-81-8435-272-6

Printed in India

Published by Harish Chandra Yadav for Adhyayan Publishers & Distributors, Laser Typeseting at A.V. Rao and Printed at Tarun Offset Printers, Delhi

ACKNOWLEDGEMENTS

I offer sincere gratitude to Dr. A. K. Awasthi, Professor and head, Dr. B. I. Guru and Dr. Nivedita Maitra of the Department of English and other European Languages, Dr. Hari Singh Gour Central University, Sagar (M.P.) for their inspiring, cooperative and encouraging attitude.

The work undertaken has made me experience many ups and downs, although I had been living with it days and nights. But there are some people who have knowingly or unknowingly figured a major role in its completion. My Papa, Mr. Tulsi Ram Tripathi, plays the role of guiding spirit behind each and every work which I undertake and accomplish. If I am in this field, it is just because of him. I am extremely thankful to him for being a constant source of encouragement and inspiration to me. I acknowledge my indebtedness from the innermost recess of my heart to husband Mr. Umakant Rajoriya for having performed various invaluable tasks, ranging from the secretarial to the menial. It is really difficult to find words to thank my family members who have always been walking on my side for anything and everything. I would also like to thank Rameti, who is like an elder daughter to me for happily taking care not only of my daughter but also me and my family throughout the work.

Finally, most important thanks here go to my little daughter Manhavi, for giving me the space and energy required to finish the work in time.

Above all it is the Almighty God whose blessings made the completion of this work possible.

PREFACE

Lawrence's work by its very nature and complexity runs the risk of being misread and misinterpreted. So, it comes as no surprise that Lawrence is one of the few writers in English literature whose work generated so much of controversy and, at the same time, scholarly work. However, it is an irony that Lawrence wrote unremittingly for upward of a quarter of a century, his work was largely ignored, except as scandal, during his life time and for many years after his death. As a result he was denied his rightful place among the literary pantheon for a long time, till F.R. Leavis put him in "the great tradition".

Lady Chatterley's lover was certainly, for the most part, misunderstood. It had always been a subject for music hall sniggering. The novel was taken as an encouragement to talk more openly about copulation, and by these who have not read it, as a sort of Bible of the new religion of promiscuity. The true essence of the book was willfully ignored.

Lawrence was described as sex prophet, voice of natural man, a willful and foolish rejecter of both science and religion. But his intensely moral vision obviates any of these categorizations. He was too great a writer to be relegated to a slot. Lawrence was acutely aware of the existing polarities between man and man, between man and society and between man and cosmos. He, therefore, committed himself to a cause to his people, to his social environment, to awaken the emotional conscience of mankind – for due to the intensity and purpose of his belief, it was not possible for him to escape in the ivory tower of pure art.

Lawrence was convinced that the western civilization constitutes the denial of life. It is repressive for it sacrifices the body to the mind, the present to the future, spontaneity to foresight and happiness to progress. Lawrence offers a non-repressive alternative to the Western cul-de-sac. I have attempted to show that Lawrence's alternative vision is rooted in an un-self-conscious acceptance of the erotic and aggressive instinct and in a living awareness of the non-human universe.

Lawrence's novels are, in the Arnoldian sense, "a criticism of life", insisting on real and living values. They have a corrective moral effect as they revive individual's capacity for direct, pre-mental responses. His art chiefly focuses on the recesses of individual consciousness, where characters encounter their generic natural self and make a crucial adjustment to it. Lawrence's novels thus become psychoanalytical novels not only in nature and technique but also in their shaping. Though a confirmed moralist, his moral ideas on life as well as on art are unconventional. In this work, I have endeavoured to prove that Lawrence was essentially a psychological novelist writing with a socio-moral purpose.

—Author

CONTENTS

1

D.H. LAWRENCE: AN INTRODUCTION

David Herbert Lawrence (1885–1930) is one of the foremost men of letters of twentieth century. Born in 1885 at Eastwood, a colliery village in Nottinghamshire, D.H. Lawrence lived in a period – 1885 to 1930, which experienced frightening changes from a world of apparent order and contentment to a world of chaos and weak nerves.

Three years before the First World War Lawrence published his first novel. His last came out in 1930; and in the twenty years between an old world broke up in violence and suffering greater than any mankind had known before. It is surprising how little of this is reflected in the great imaginative literature of the period. The novel especially is supposed to hold the mirror to the times; yet from the work of Lawrence's great contemporaries– Gide, Proust, Mann and Joyce – a reader from another planet would hardly gather much of the convulsion in Europe. Perhaps it is so usually minor literature that reflects history in any immediately recognizable way. The tempests of the imagination are not those, which vex the sea of political history. It is in the work of Lawrence, too. A chapter of Kangaroo and a handful of letters reveal his response to the war-a-response so egoistical as to be almost insane. He has an intense private concern with class distinctions, but almost none with the functioning class system and the transformations it was going through in his lifetime. The old social edifice, patched and factory and slum, was to be swept down the flood before his eyes; but his life as an artist goes on almost independently of all this. The fact is that for him, as for most of the great imaginative writers of the time, the historical catastrophe was only part of a great revolution of sensibility; a revolution that began before the political ones, and may be uncompleted yet, though it seems to have reached at least a temporary point of rest. In this great change of feeling, indescribable while it was taking place, yet cumulatively so distinctive, between the pre-1914 world and our own, Lawrence is surely very near the center.

If descriptions given in his novels are relied upon, it can be said that he came into the world under the sign of hatred. His mother "dreaded this baby like a catastrophe, because of her feelings for her husband." When only two weeks old he developed bronchitis. In Sons and Lovers we have the following passage describing that his mother feared he was "unhealthy or malformed".

> ....she noticed the peculiar knitting of the baby's brows and the peculiar heaviness of its eyes as if it were trying to understand something that was pain. She felt when she looked at the child's dark, brooding pupils, as if a burden were on her heart............With all her force, with all her soul she would make up to it for having brought it into the world unloved. She would love it all the more now it was here; carry it in her love.[1]

When an infant, his surprised and brooding eyes suggested to his mother some sort of predestination. Mrs. Lawrence named him after David, the predestined Biblical shepherd boy, with whom Lawrence was to identify himself on occasions more than one. His intense affection for his mother, his sadness during his father's bouts of drunkenness, his anxiety in the face of ever-present threat of an accident in the mine, his fragile health with weak chest were the traits of Herbert Lawrence as reflected in his autobiographical novel, Sons and Lovers through the character of Paul Morel:

> As a rule he seemed old for his years. He was so conscious of what other people felt, particularly his mother. When she fretted he understood and could have no peace. His soul seemed always attentive to her.[2]

Lawrence's father and mother were temperamentally poles apart. The unabated warfare between the parents had its adverse affect on children. As Lawrence grew up he was forced to consider the relationship between men and women as a form of conflict, not a natural expression of harmony.

Professionally Lawrence's first work was published in 1909, when in the November issue of the English Review a group of his poem under the general title of "A Still Afternoon" was printed. Jessie Chambers, with whom Lawrence was infatuated in his early years, sent these poems to the editor, Ford Mādox Hucffer (later Ford Madox Ford.). Lawrence later on wrote. "The girl-had launched me so easily, on my literary career, like a princess cutting a thread, launching a ship. Lawrence was inherently a poet, and so when he took to writing he was absorbed in the emotional and imaginative element of the individual. When he came to London as a schoolmaster, in 1908 at the age of twenty-three, he brought the manuscript of a novel, The White Peacock, on which he had been working for several years, and it was published in 1911. Told by an onlooker narrator, it centers upon the gradual breakdown of a farmer's son after a girl he loves has rejected him in favour of a richer suitor. Lawrence at this time admired the works of George Eliot, and the chief distinction of his book from hers is the use of English rural scenery to heighten the emotional atmosphere, though his poetic rhythms and images produce a more opulent effect than did her pedestrian style. In displaying a man's disintegration resulting from subservience to a selfish woman, the book established Lawrence's principal theme.

The originality of style in "The white peacock", and Lawrence's personal charm, brought him friends among the young writers in London, and when illness compelled him to give up teaching they helped him to earn a meager income by writing. His second novel The Trespasser is inferior to his first, the descriptive. Its passages being turgidly overwritten. Again the theme is a woman's destructive rejection of her lover, and the erotic element pervades the book.

At this juncture Lawrence's own emotional life under went a change. Hitherto he had been dominated by a possessive mother his (Lawrence's) parents marriage had not been a success. The mother, who came of a family with some pretensions to culture and refinement, was attracted to a coalminer of vitality and possessing a full share of earthy gaiety and abounding spirits, but withal rough and uncouth and sullenly resentful of the superior attainments of his wife. But this union led to the disaster which later on became the major theme of all of the Lawrence's novels. Lawrence say's of her:

> The pity was she was too much his opposite. She could not be content with the little he might be; she would have him the much that he ought to be. So, in seeking to make him nobler than he could be, she destroyed him. She injured and scarred herself, but she lost none of her worth.[3]

As Lawrence grew up he was forced to consider the relationship between men and women as a form of conflict, not a natural expression of harmony. Moreover, if we are to believe Lawrence, his mother, disappointed in her husband, turned to her son for the satisfaction and understanding she failed to find in her marriage. The strain that this implied relationship imposed on his adolescent emotions can be seen in his abnormal sensitivity to any threatened domination by women and the almost hysterical violence with which he countered it.

Lawrence's devotion to his mother had caused a breach with a girl who attracted him and who had helped him to develop his literary talent, and Mrs. Lawrence's death, just at the time his first novel came out, plunged him into despair. A year later, however, he fell in love with the wife of one of his former professors, four years older than he, and the mother of several children. Together they went to the continent to meet her family, who were of the German nobility, and wandered there for a year, during which he finished revising a novel that dealt directly with his own early life. The decisive break with his past enabled him to look at it with understanding and detachment.

The title Sons and Lovers, clearly states the book's psychological theme. The technique is more strictly realistic than in his first two novels, presenting the coalmining village of his childhood as objectively as Bennett depicted Hanley. Paul Morel's drunken but likable father and his stubborn mother are portraits of Lawrence's parents. The mother's control over the sex life of her son drives the elder to involvement with a mistress and then to physical breakdown and death. The younger son Paul loves Miriam Leavers, a strong minded girl, who tries vainly to break his bondage to his mother. After separating from Miriam, Paul has an affair with a married woman, and this time

emotional crises are conveyed in a series of prose-poems, through which Lawrence seeks to suggest a mystical theory that sexual gratification has to be transmuted into some sort of spiritual union. He is transferring into an entirely emotional realm the theme that Meredith had expounded in term of woman's need for instinctual independence. The essence of Lawrence as a mythopoeic creative artist is contained in the last paragraphs of The Rainbow:

> "In everything she was she grasped and groped to find the creation of the living god, instead of the old, hard barren forms of bygone living. Sometimes great terror possessed her. Sometimes she lost touch, she lost her feeling, she could only know the old horror of the husk which is bound in her and all mankind. They were all in prison, they were all going mad.

She saw the stiffened bodies of the colliers, which seemed already enclosed in a coffin, she was sick with a nausea so deep that she perished as she sake. And then, in the blowing clouds, she saw a band of faint iridescence colouring in faint colour a portion of the hill. And forgetting, startled, she looked for the covering colour and saw a rainbow forming itself. In one place it gleamed fiercely and her heart anguished with hope, she sought the shadow of iris where the bow should be. Steadily the colours gathered, mysteriously, from nowhere it took presence upon itself, there was a taint, vast rainbow.

> She knew that the sordid people who crept hard-scaled and separate on the face of the world's corruption were living still, that The Rainbow was arched in their blood and would quiver to life in their spirit, that they would cast off their horny covering of disintegration, that new, clean, naked bodies would issue to a new germination, to a new growth, rising to the light and the wind and the old brittle corruption

> of houses and factories swept away, the world built up in a living fabric of truth, fitting to the over-arching heaven.[5]

When published in 1915, The Rainbow was assailed in the press for indecency and was suppressed. The outcry was directed against the frank description of physical intimacies and particularly a lesbian episode that occurs at one stage of Ursula's search for a solution to her sexual agonies. Defiantly Lawrence went on to write a sequel, Women in Love, which was even more explicit in its erotic scenes. Ursula now finds a satisfactory partner in Philip Birkin, who represents Lawrence's own conception of sex, and their love story is contrasted with two other, one of which fails because it is confined to immediate gratification of desire, and the other because the woman is the dominant personality. S. Diana Neill in his book 'A short History of the English Novel' has given some fine observation on this book to quote the following lines for instance:

> The style of the book is singularly fluid and unrestrained and often marred by inartistic repetition of words and phrases. The chief characters are not seen from the outside and "in the round" but are realized from within as vortices of electro magnetic energy alternately attracting and repelling. Never had the obscure antagonism between sexes that has its origin, perhaps, in some unknown, little understood nerve centers of the body been so vividly described. Running through the book is a vein of exciting kinesthetic imagery that can turn the simple gesture of throwing a stone at the moon mirrored in a pond into a cosmic art.
>
> For Lawrence nothing was inanimate, life quivered and surged in everything around him, and throughout the entire creation he sought for signs of the eternal polarities – light and darkness, male and female, love and hate.[6]

When no publisher would incur the risk of bringing the book out, it was privately printed in 1920, and provoked a new wave of censure for containing recognizable and mainly unflattering portraits of some of Lawrence's friends.

By this time the Lawrence's living were in Italy, and his impressions of the Mediterranean landscape are to be found in his next novel, The lost Girl (1920) couched in his most charming vein of poetic description. Otherwise the book is undistinguished, and it suffers from diffuseness of scene, as it ranges from a draper's shop in a mining town through a student nurse's hospital experience to her life in Italy as the wife of an actor. She is a feminine counterpart of the young men in the realistic novels of Bennett Wells, and Maugham, and the sexual element was so much less offensive than in Lawrence's preceding books that this one was awarded a major British prize as the best novel of the year.

In Lawrence's later works the poetry was painfully at war with the nomiletics. In search of a climate beneficial for his tuberculosis, and of some mode of consciousness free from modern tensions, the Lawrence's ranged restlessly from the Mediterranean to Ceylon, Australia, and Mexico, until they found the best conditions in the New Mexican desert. The setting of his novels record the stages of the pilgrimage, Aaron's Rod (1992), which is partly autobiographical in its portrayal of a mine worker with Musical gifts, is a loosely constructed story that moves from England to Florence. Aaron Sisson deserts the wife whom he loves; because he feels instinctively that she is engulfing him, and he eventually finds a man friend Raw don Lilly, who becomes the persons of Lawrence in the later part of the book, struggling to redeem Aaron by his gospel of the "power motive..... Not intellectual power. Not mental power. Not conscious will power. Not even wisdom. But dark, living, fructifying power."[7]

The self-portraiture is even more faithful in his Australian novel, Kangaroo (1923), in which the hero is a bearded English author, disillusioned by wartime persecution, who seeks isolation in Australia but becomes involved in fascist and socialist organizations. The subsequent Riots and Violence are uncomfortably prescient of the disturbances that were soon to beset the world. Lawrence's obsession with power weighs heavily on the book, and the hero's soliloquies reiterate his doctrine that "the only thing one can stick to is ones own isolate being, and the god in whom it is rooted. And the only thing to look to is the god who fulfils one from the dark."

Another novel with an Australian setting, The Boy in the Bush, is Lawrence's rewriting of a manuscript by a woman whom he met there. Then his visit to Mexico produced the most horrifying of his novels on the theme of power, The Plumed Serpent (1926). The ancient Aztec cults satisfied his craving for a primitive frame of reference posited upon the elemental instincts. A cultivated Irish widow marries an Indian general who participates in a revolution dedicated to ousting Christianity from the country in favour of the old gods, and democracy in favour of the old gods, and democracy in favour of a fascist dictatorship. Some where, Lawrence believed that at some point in our development we humans had taken a wrong turning and consequently we had tried through the centuries to live according to an unavailing theory—Christianity—which denied the wholeness of man and falsely renounced the primal source of consciousness in nature. The theme of the novel is the revolt of the native population of Mexico in favour of the old Aztec gods, whose cult is revived with ceremonial magic and mythopoeic hymns.

The plumed serpent showed Lawrence's preoccupation with the great cosmic laws underlying sex relationships to which all other aspects of life are lined by restoring mans supremacy and in giving woman fulfillment within her own world of physical consciousness he believed the neurotic restlessness of the modern world could be overcome.

In this novel Lawrence's descriptive power is at its apex in his representation of the brilliant, crude clamors of the Mexican scene, the filth and terror, the ferocity and bloodshed of a bullfight and of a bandit foray. The leader of the revolution indulges in mystical exercises reminiscent of Eastern Yogi, and the three principal characters go through a ritual of initiation as reincarnations of the Aztec gods.

Lawrence's favourable portrayal of autocratic leaders in Kangaroo and The Plumed serpent seems to reflect his own ambition to initiate a movement toward a Utopia of emotionally liberated souls. His declining health, and the failure of his admirers to join him in avant grade colony in Laos, put an end to this phase. He began to realize that social revolution entailed militancy, whereas his dream was for a sensitive and tender understanding between individuals. Therefore, the Plumed Serpent marks the close of his glorification of power, and his next novel concentrated upon his other persistent theme, sex. In Lady Chatterley's lover (1928) he reiterated his lifelong concern over the sexual dilemma – mans physical need for woman and his equally compulsive need for spiritual independence from her. With this theory he merged his theory that men are superior to the effect products of culture because they follow the normal human impulses without perversion or shame. He returned to the English rural setting of his early novels and told the story of an aristocratic woman who is driven to seek sexual gratification surreptitiously because her husband is paralyzed by wartime injuries. After an unsatisfactory affair with a young playwright, she discovers the beauty and joy of honest passion with a virile gamekeeper. It is true that Mellor's has obtained an education for himself, but he is essentially a representative of the lowest social class, as Lawrence idealized it, sensitively loving the beauty of nature and frankly obeying his primitive instincts.

Lawrence considered this to be the most effective manifesto of his doctrine, and he wrote the whole book three times, achieving a unity and a sense of inevitable destiny that contrasted with the lax structure of most of his novels. The original draft, which was printed in 1944 and the first Lady Chatterley, is shallower and emotionally less tense than the final rewriting. The explicit record of sexual inter course places the book in the tradition of naturalism; but Lawrence endured it with his idealistic mission of rescuing the physical function of sex from infamy by depicting it as beautiful. Because he flagrantly employed vulgar words that are seldom seen in print, and because his familiar geographical and social details were less efficient than the exotic environments of his preceding novels in veiling the lewdness of the events, he incurred the old accusation of immorality, and for the second time one of his books was legally suppressed as obscene. Until 1959 the edition's available in the United States were a censored version made after the authors death. His only subsequent novel, The Virgin and the Gypsy, which has a similar theme, was unfinished when he died in 1930, and was printed from his manuscript draft.

Just before the end of his life Lawrence put his theory into an exquisite parable, The Man Who Died (1931). This sensitive study possesses a lyric beauty that is enhanced by the cool nervous prose in which the parable; describing the union of the two great religions which have divided the world, Christianity and the mother-cult-of Isis, is expressed.

Lawrence was hostile to Christianity because for two thousand years it had glorified the ascetic life and taught that the flesh was unholy. To him flesh and spirit were one and division was evil. In the story Christ does not die upon the cross, but is nursed back to health by a peasant and his wife. During the period in which he sits recuperating in the bright sunshine, he realizes that it is not enough to have died for man, that he must live for him, and this new awareness leads him to leave the peasants and make his way to the Temple of Isis. There he encounters Isis, the moon goddess, queen of the dark mysteries of the underworld, the spouse of the sun-god. The priestess in the temple is an incarnation of the goddess and she brings to the restored Christ an understanding of the vital mystery of life. At least the consummation is complete and the harmony between flesh and spirit is finally achieved.

Lawrence was the only novelist of his time to use the novel for the purpose of re-creating the great myths by which humanity lives, and he did it with a burning intensity and sincerity. His prose style matched his strange vision. Its dark radiance sprang from a poetic fervor that found expression in words and phrases charged with suggestive beauty. Yet the fact that he was attempting to convey a meaning that is only truly explicit in symbols led to an intolerable amount of repetition and diffusiveness. He often seems to be suffocating in his effort to express the visions of his brain. The "personal factor" to which reference has been made, and the absence of any formal literary culture, may have been to blame for the laboured eroticism of the novels. But when all is said there is greatness in him, he is something of an authentic visionary, and the future may be in a better position to interpret his dreams.

Lawrence was no experimenter in technique as Legouis and Cazamians puts it:

> D.H. Lawrence has not been a creator of forms. His originality was content to use with impatient vigor such instruments as he found ready to his hand. His novels, the realism of which is all stirred by a longing for symbolical suggestion, will glow now and again with poetic ardours; but their informing thought is not strong enough, nor is their structure sufficiently firm to check, a tendency to diffusion and disorder; their method of insistence and repetition is some what over emphatic and heavy..... the artist in him is neither very great nor of the finest quality; Lawrence indeed would not rank so high as he does, but for the somebre enthusiasm that raises him above his own self. Nor is his teaching other than a disappointment to those who expect from it an answer to the anxieties of our age. One cannot take very seriously a dislike for modern civilization that harks back to the simplest modes of life, without finding in them any genuine refreshment; a thirst for the untried and the exotic which every satisfaction leaves unshaken and embittered; a skepticism enamored of vague mystic imaginings; a religion of physical love shot through and through with the consciousness of its fragility. Nevertheless, owing to that very anarchy of purpose, to those wild outbursts of despair as much as of desire, Lawrence's work is among those in which the men and women of our time have found their own restlessness most accurably mirrored; and however unequal, feverish, morbid that work may be, it possesses an energy of impassioned imagination which stamps it with the characteristics marks of greatness.[8]

To conclude we can say that Lawrence's works will probably owe their lasting interest to the rich significant confession of his tragic spiritual fate; they will live, moreover, in a series of beautiful fragments, close grim pictures of miners' or peasants' homes, scenes of English provincial life, studies in unsettled sensibilities, of crisis in adolescence, images of distant lands of sunshine and death, unforgettable outpourings of the solitary or the enslaved soul. The next age may find in them a type of the chaos rather than of the moral liberation of ours; and clear testimony to the active presence of the new psychology in the intellectual background of the last twenty years; Lawrence intuitively discovered that doctrine as much as he became acquainted with it in the usual way, and the sense of a dark edge to the lights of the inner world is conspicuous through all his utterances, setting of each phrase with a depth and a shadow.

NOTES AND REFERENCES

1. D.H. Lawrence, *Sons and Lovers*, London, 1956, http://www.fullbooks.com/Sons-and-Lovers-by-David-Herbert-Lawrence-D.html.
2. D.H. Lawrence, *Sons and Lovers*, London, 1956, http://www.fullbooks.com/Sons-and-Lovers-by-David-Herbert-Lawrence-D.html.
3. D.H. Lawrence, *Sons and Lovers*, London, 1956, http://www.fullbooks.com/Sons-and-Lovers-by-David-Herbert-Lawrence-D.html.
4. *The Collected Letters of D.H. Lawrence*, ed, Harry T. moore (2vols) Lodon (Heinemann) 1962, p. 291.
5. Omendra Sinha, *D. H. Lawrence: The Prophet of New Life and Art*, National Publishing House, New Delhi, 1997, pp. 997, pp.31
6. D.H. Lawrence, *The Rainbow*, London, 1955, http://www.archive.org/details/rainbow00lawrgoog.
7. S. Diana Neill, *A Short History of the English Novel*, London, 1953.
8. Legouis and Cazamians, *History of English Literature*, Macmillan India ltd., 1995, pp. 1359-60.

2

LAWRENCE'S MORAL CONCERNS AND PSYCHOANALYSIS

From the middle of the nineteenth century onward, the strongest influence upon the novel was exerted by science First the evolutionary biologists implanted the idea that man must be regarded as a specially developed genus of animal and therefore in fiction the naturalists interpreted human behaviour on the basis of primitive instincts. Then the social scientists emphasized the structure of society and the psychological importance of the environment, and therefore the later realists examined man in his familial and cultural groups. By the end of the century a new branch of science focused attention on the individual, when Sigmund Freud developed his methods of revealing the unconscious spring of action.

This problem had always been of paramount importance to novelist. From Richardson onward, they had tried to find a convincing way to display a character's inner reactions as well as his overt conduct. Most of them were hampered by the assumption that "thought" was always rational, and could be conveyed in logical predications. Hence came the implausible formality of passages enclosed in quotation marks and labeled, "he said to himself." When Dickens occasionally departed from this convention, as in the dreams and hallucinations of Skies, and Fagin, Jonas, Chuzzlewit and Tigg, he was accused of being melodramatic and Fantastic. But as the news from Freud's Clinic came to public attention in the early years of the twentieth century, some novelists realized that this might provide tools they had been seeking.

The naturalists were vindicated so far as their concentration upon irrational motives went, but their narrative method with its scientific logic, was obviated by the new attention to dreams and uncontrolled reverie, "The novelist who marks the transition from naturalism to psychoanalysis is David Herbert Lawrence. His first successful novel "Sons and Lover's" dealing with the Oedipus complex gave Lawrence the status of having written the first psychoanalytical novel in the English language.

Psychological Novel can be defined as a prose fiction that places unusual emphasis on interior characterization and on the motives, circumstances, and internal action that spring from, and develop external action. The psychological novel not content to state what happens goes on to explain the why of this action:

> Lawrence has always been something of a problem to the critic; if one, to think of him as primarily an artist, or essentially a moralist, or both. Should one discuss him as a novelist in a tradition? If so, is that tradition to be that of the English novel, or a larger European tradition? Or is he, more than a writer in a certain tradition, on innovator, a "tablet breaker", a rebel? Or again is he both? To what extent is Lawrence an autobiographical writer and what effect has this on his work as a novelist? Can one completely divorce Lawrence the man from his work and consider his novels purely as self-sufficient works of art? How far was Lawrence a psychoanalytical writer? How

> much a symbolist?........... These are some of the questions critics of Lawrence have found themselves faced with, and which they have, in their own ways, tried to answer though neither, it must be said, with much success nor consistence........ There is surely, as a rule, more than one legitimate, and fruitful, approach to any great writer. But whether a critic sets out to discuss a writer's work as "art" on the basis of some aesthetic theory, or seeks to bring out its significance in terms of human values, there is little justification for any literary criticism that does not help deepen our understanding or increase our enjoyment of creative literary works. A large proportion of Lawrence criticism, owing to its failure to recognize the essential in Lawrence, does neither.[1]

Lawrence was essentially a socio-moral novelist and to achieve his end or aim he practiced the method of psychoanalysis. To understand the psychoanalytical method employed by Lawrence we must know what exactly is meant by the psychological novel and how one should approach it. Leon Edel, in his book, "The psychological novel" has explained very nicely what exactly is meant by the psychological novel. To quote from this book:

> In the old novels the second voice of Mr. Eliot's definition was always heard. The omniscient author was nearly always present and nearly always addressing an audience. Perhaps for the purposes of fiction, we can put it in another way in the old novels we are nearly always seated face to face with the author, it is he who is looking out of the window and telling us the story of what he sees.... However much, we would like to go and take a look out of the window ourselves we cannot do so, because the omniscient author is occupying the choice seat.... In the psychological novel

the author is nowhere in sight. Suddenly we are seated at the window. Somewhere, above, behind, below, out beyond the window the author is busy being a stage manager and an actor, arranging what we shall see. He tries to give us the illusion constantly that we are experiencing what is happening there, and in the process he asks us to look at all sorts of extraneous things, strange things, as if we were in one of our own dreams in which impossible and implausible events occur magical transformations, return of episodes and people out of forgotten pasts,..... before, we forget ourselves out there amid the confusion, living all that the writer has arranged for us. From being listeners once removed from the scene, we have become actual participants.....We must recognize, however, that he forces nothing upon us; it rests with us, if we wish, to make, effort to discover whether communication with him is at all possible.... Both readers and critics who have insistently asked the psychological novelist to mend his ways and revert to old methods and old forms have failed to recognize the collaborative nature of novel reading. The argument advanced by certain of our less perceptive critics that there was no justification for attempting to discover new techniques to render subjective experience when the traditional mode of narration has so richly served us, is so much an appeal for turning novel into something rigid and static that it can only be dismissed as puerile.

It is critics too who have tended to regard the psychological novel as morbid, because it goes into the mind and explores "unhealthy" areas of experience. They often argue that the subjective novel springs from incapacitated person, Lawrence and his Oedipus complex, Proust and his asthma, Joyce and his near-

> How does my cat recognize me in the dark? – Ugh, thank God there are more and other sorts of vision that the Kodak sort which Mr. Muir esteems above all others.[4]

Lawrence's vision strips away appearances, even personalities, and penetrates into being. Just as Carlyle, for all his provincialism and eccentricity, gains strength from taking part in a general European movement against mechanism and materialism, so Lawrence, for all his rejections and rootlessness, gains strength from taking part in the great European expedition away from the usual trade – routes into the hinterland of consciousness. And that is where any consideration of his work as a novelist must ultimately arrive. Lawrence continually enlarges the boundaries of our consciousness, and a judgment of his individual artistic achievement will in the long run probably depend on the extent and the worth of the new territory acquired. Of course with many novelists this kind of inquiry would be pointless. They are concerned with putting in order experiences of a king we are already quite familiar with. Lawrence (or Dostoevsky or, in his own way Proust) extends our experience; and to think about a novelist of this kind at once lands us in difficulties. We cannot talk for long about techniques, powers of representation or even of moral insight, for we soon find that we are dealing with ideas and mental states that we have never clearly recognized till we meet them in this particular artistic content. Murray wrote to Frieda in 1953: 'Why, half the Rainbow was completely beyond myken when it was published' (Ibid 330). Murray saw quicker than most the immense superiority of Lawrence to the other writers of the time. Yet, by all the accepted cannons, his work was flawed, Murray was forced into a false choice between Lawrence and art. He chose Lawrence:

> Much better 'art' has been produced by Lawrence's contemporaries; books better shaped, novels more objectively conceived, poems more concentrated. Beside Lawrence's work they seem frigid and futile.[5]

Lawrence's greatness is attributed to the fact that 'at bottom' he was not concerned with art.

> He gave up, deliberately, the pretence of being an artist. The novel became for him simply a means by which he could make explicit his own thought–adventures'...... His aim was to discover authority, not to create art.

Murry here comes to the very brink of understanding, but turns aside into Chaos:

> But not a great artist. He was a prophet, a psychologist, a philosopher, what you will—but more than any other single thing, the great life adventurer of modern times. If Lawrence is 'what you will', he is vulnerable to all the subjective criticism anyone cares to level at him.[6]

'Destructive hagiography' is Aldous Huxley's phrase for Murray's criticism. He constructs an apparatus of psychology-cum-gossip to account for Lawrence's work and to evaluate it in inverse ratio to its merit as art. Neither Murray, nor Eliot, nor even Leavis, could see what Lawrence 'was after' during his life time. Their complaints that Lawrence is not always objective or impersonal enough an artist or that he occasionally violates the cannon of aesthetic distance in his novels or that he is a sex prophet—these complaints, we shall see, are based on a static, fixed conception of what a novel is, or ought to be.

All the aesthetic criticism of Lawrence is based on a narrow, fixed conception of art. It takes for granted certain rules or principles as axiomatic. But there are not, there cannot be, any fixed, static principles of literary criticism valid for all time. Any really great writer forces us, in one way or another, to reconsider and extend our ideas about the nature and function of literary art and its forms. Applying irrelevant aesthetic principles to Lawrence's novels serves not the least purpose. Lawrence was an avowedly moral writer moral in the widest and best sense of the term. He believed that his genius was essentially religious, and that he wrote from a deep moral sense. He was impatient of art "too much cooked in the artistic consciousness". He did not, he declared, "care a button" for neat works of art. Writing to the Italian critic Carlo Linati, Lawrence said:

> But really, Signor Linati, do you think that books should be sort of toys, nicely built up of observations and sensations, all finished and complete? I don't .... I can't bear art that you can walk round and admire. A book should be either a bandit or a rebel or a man in a crowd. People should either run for their lives, or come under the colours, or say how do you do? I hate the actor-and-the-audience business. An author should be in among the crowd, kicking their shins or cheering on to some mischief or merriment. That rather cheap seat in the gods where one sits with fellows like Anatole France and benignly looks down on the foibles, Follies, and Frenzies of so-called fellow-men, just annoys me. After all, the world is not a stage-not to me, nor a theatre, nor a show house of any sort. And art, especially novels, are not like theatres where the reader sits aloft and watches – like a god with a twenty – lira ticket and sighs, commiserates, condones and smiles. That's what you want a book to be, because it leaves you so safe and so superior, with you two-dollar ticket to the show.

> And that's what my books are not and never will be. You need not complain that I don't subject the intensity of my vision-or whatever it is – to some vast and imposing rhythm – by which you mean, isolate it on a state, so that you can look down on it like a god who has got a ticket to the show, I never will... whoever reads me will be in the thick of the scrimmage, and if he doesn't line it – if he wants a safe seat in the audience-let him read somebody else.[7]

Lawrence was essentially a moralist. With scant regard for the aesthetic doctrines of the "artistic anarchists" who make art out of antipathy of life, he wrote with a deep moral sense. For him writing was a part of his commitment to make the human life most deeply alive. To this end he constantly endeavoured to create a new world of psychically liberated sensual experience. He believes in the innate goodness of the individual self and allies his art with polemical attempt to involve the reader in his didactics "Whoever reads me will be in thick of the scrimmage," he warned, "and if he doesn't like it, if he wants safe seat in the audience, let him read somebody else."[8]

Lawrence was both an artist and a prophet at once, and his moral intention and his art are inextricably bound up together. Explaining his views on the relation of art and morality, Lawrence wrote:

> The essential function of art is moral. Not aesthetic, not decorative, not pastime and recreation. But a passionate implicit morality; a morality which changes the blood, rather that the mind. Changes the blood first, the mind follows later, in the wake.[9]

It is well to remember the distinction Lawrence makes here between implicit passionate morality and didactic morality, because, while he does not believe that a work of art is immoral just because the artist has any dominant idea or purpose, the immorality comes in when the artist puts his thumb in the scale to pull it down in favour of his didactic purpose – which is quite often directly opposed to his personal inspiration. Art, in a way is utterly dependent on the artist's vision of life for philosophy, (or "metaphysic") – even if the artist is at first not conscious of it. Every work of art "adheres to some system of morality." But, adds Lawrence, if it is really a work of art, it must contain the essential criticism of this morality to which it adheres; for while all systems of morality are of temporary value, useful to their times.

> Art must give a deeper satisfaction......The degree to which the system of morality, or the metaphysic, of any work of art is submitted to criticism within the work of art makes the lasting value and satisfaction of the work.[10]

As a human being Lawrence had his own views about what life should be like, and how this could be brought about. But his conclusions are not offered as conclusions of the novels. It is ridiculous to pass moral judgments on Lawrence's social, political, or philosophical ideas and offer these as valid literary criticism of the novels. But while there is no justification for bringing in Lawrence's beliefs stated outside his fiction in order to arrive at literary judgements on their basis, these views are undoubtedly helpful in trying to clarify Lawrence's meaning. No adequate literary criticism of Lawrence can even begin without a proper understanding of Lawrence's closely connected ideas about art, morality, life, human relationships and the conflicts inherent in them.

Lawrence's dictum that the essential function of art is moral becomes clearer when we see the close correspondence between his views on art and on morality. "Art", he says "displays.......living conjunction between the self and its content", whereas for him the "essence of morality is the basic desire to preserve the perfect correspondence between the self and the object......" The business of art is "to reveal the relation between man and his circumbient universe"[11], while morality is that delicate, changing balance between man and the circumbient universe which accompanies this relatedness. Art reveals things in their different relationships. The relation between the things changes from day to day. Therefore art which reveals these changing relations is forever new.

> Morality for Lawrence is not a set of rules or prescriptions. On the contrary, he characterizes morality based on ideas and ideals as "unmitigated evil". Morality, pure morality, is only "an instinctive adjustment which the soul makes in every circumstance, adjusting one thing to another livingly, delicately, sensitively". Anything that damages this delicate adjustment is sinful and immoral. Our main business is to be fully, vividly alive. That which brings into us a stronger and deeper flow of life is good and moral, that which impairs this flow is evil. "There is only one sin in life, and that is the sin against life."
>
> **Evil, What is evil?**
>
> Here is only one evil, to deny life........(Poems II, p. 525) To sacrifice oneself to anything or anybody whatsoever is the vilest deed a man can do, "....the vilest cowardice and treachery". As to saving one's soul, how and why should the soul be "saved"? One can save one's pennies, Lawrence remarks, but how can one save one's soul? One can only live one's soul. The business is to live, be really alive. Real living is the only truth. "The problem of truth is" how can we most deeply live?

A man can, of course, do nothing with his life but live it: but every man has to learn to be himself, his real spontaneous self.....one cannot, however, live in sheer full spontaneity by one's instincts alone, there must be a "perfect harmony between the conscious intelligence and the unconscious, preconscious prompting......" ....Living consists in doing what the life in us really wants to do, not what the ego imagines we want to do, And to find out how the life in us wants to be lived is terribly difficult......A things isn't "life" just because somebody does it, and an artist ought to know this perfectly well.

The ordinary bank clerk buying himself a new straw hat isn't life at all: it is just existence, quite all right, like everyday dinners; but not "life".

By life we mean something that gleams that has the fourth dimensional quality. If the bank clerk feels really piquant about his hat, if he establishes a lively relation with it, and goes out of the shop with the new straw on his head, a changed man, be-aurcoled, then that is life.....When an artist or a novelist writes about this transformation in the bank-clerk, he writes of "life".... It is Lawrence's constant, persistent concern with, and exultance in, life as lived in individual beings which made one critic remark that Lawrence was "terribly, over whelmingly in love with life".

...............Lawrence was a living man, and he transmitted the life in him through his creative works by ....kindling the life quality where it was not. It was his belief that all work done with real interest, all creative work, becomes fountain of life for others. In one of his letters he defined a hero as one who touches and transmits the life of the universe. This is what his own work pre-eminently does..........

> There is hardly any man living. Lawrence says in "We Need One Another". Who can exist at all cheerfully without a relationship to some particular woman; and there is hardly a woman on earth who can live, cheerfully without some intimate relationship to a man. Men and women have their true being only when they are related, in contact they are not separate entities in themselves.......... Love between man and woman, when it is whole, is both sacred and profane, spiritual as well as sensual .... The aim in man-woman relationship, then, is the attainment of a balance between love and individuality, between spiritual and sensual consummation............ Lawrence's primary concern in his novels is to help us live, by revealing to us our life as a series of living, changing relationships with all the conflicts inherent in them.[12]

All his (Lawrence's) novels are essentially, imaginative explorations of life in its various relationships. In Lawrence's novels there is some use of symbolism, a definite strain of nihilism, a certain amount of psychoanalytic writing, and much excellently done social realism. But all these are subordinate to Lawrence's main purpose, which is to reveal to us "the changing rainbow of our living relationships".[13]

In nearly all of Lawrence's works both the social and the individual morality are inextricably interwoven. According to him, art is not purely aesthetic and entertaining, but inescapably moral. Through Lawrence accepts that the essential function of art is moral he condemns the writer who writes simply for the sake of purpose or philosophy. He avers that "the adherence to metaphysics does not necessarily give artistic form. Indeed, the over strong adherence to a metaphysics usually destroys any possibility of artistic form. A work of art attains its true "from" only when it imparts the reader a fairly "deep and comprehensive satisfaction". Thus the complete submission of a work of art to metaphysic or morality has scarcely any artistic worth. As a matter of fact, Lawrence asserts, a good work of art should not merely adhere to a certain morality, is of temporary value, while art is of external value. In the incomplete, long critical essay, "Study of Thomas hardy" he affirms: ....all morality is of temporary value, useful to its times. But art must give deeper satisfaction. It must give fair play all rounds.[14]

Yet every work of art adheres to some system of morality. But if it be really a work of art, it must contain the essential criticism on the morality to which it adheres. And hence the antimony; hence the antimony, to every tragic conception.

The degree to which the system of morality, or the metaphysic, of any work of art is submitted to criticism within the work of art makes the lasting value and satisfaction of that work.

This is the most admirable Lawrentian insight. Lawrence does not want a mere dramatic representation of two opposite ideologies in a literary work, but the subjection of the morality to which the writer adheres to essential criticism. In actual practice, an ideologically committed writer tends to depict in his work a conflict between his own ideology and its opposite, only to reveal the deficiencies of the latter and the strength of the former. This is the reason why "Much of what Lawrence says at one time he contradicts, at least superficially, at another, so that to confront him is not an easy task. "It is in some ways like tackling Coleridge or Ruskin confusion of detail, contradiction, mania, false science – yet throughout, power, and intelligence that besides penetrating to what are called the central problems of the time, casts a brilliant and arresting light on many facets of experience that have never been illuminated before. (The Dark sun, Graham Hough).[15]

Lawrence's interests are so curiously variegated that they have always run the risk of being misinterpreted and distorted. For this reason he has often been misunderstood by critics while for the most part his ideas remained incomprehensible to his readers. Nonetheless he was committed to life and health of "English folk" and exerted an influence for the same. Therefore he writes in a letter to A.W. McLeod:

> .... And I am so sure that only through a readjustment between men and women, and a making free and healthy of this sex, will she got out of her present atrophy. Oh Lord, and if a I don't "subdue my art to a metaphysic" as somebody very beautifully said of Hardy, I do write because I want folk English folk-to alter, and have more sense.[16]

Lawrence is essentially a socio-moral novelist. But his moral concept is not traditional in nature. All traditional morality is essentially sex oriented morality. And in his novels Lawrence wages a war against the traditional morality. His objective in writing such novels seems to be a challenge to the contemporary social morality. Further he is probing the moral or the subconscious of the people. What people essentially feel but are unable to act accordingly and this situation results in a deformity in behaviour or personality which if not freed from such deformation will out live to remain suppressed for ages together. Accordingly the behaviour of such a potent part of society will undergo a drastic change which will have serious repercussions. Therefore through his novels Lawrence tried to change the traditional false conception of morality. He tried to free the body and sex from the stigma of being unholy. To expose the falsity of the traditional morality Lawrence exposed the "dark core of mind of the seemingly moral individuals and their relationships. For this probing deep into the minds of the characters become necessary and therefore Lawrence practiced psychoanalysis. Therefore we can say that in writing novels Lawrence's aim was to bring about a social change and create better moral conditions. And to achieve his aim, he practiced the method of psychoanalysis. Or in other words we can say that by exposing the dark corner's of the minds of the seemingly moral character's and in this way exposing contemporary social morality Lawrence tried to achieve his aim of creating better and healthy moral conditions in the society.

In describing men and women Lawrence tried to go too far down into the dark sources of consciousness. Seeking for the fundamental springs of personality, he got below personality. His novels are full of subtle human conflicts, but they are never conflicts which particularize his characters as human beings; they are examples of passions, of states of feeling, mostly in the abstract. His people, with one or two exceptions, are merely wells or rather geysers of instinct. Acting from impulses so obscure that they dim, they don't illuminate individual. As a novelist, Lawrence's profound sensibility tended to defeat its own ends. As in an often quoted letter Lawrence has said that:

> ....that which is psychic non-human, in humanity, is more interesting to me than the old fashioned human element which causes one to conceive a character in a certain moral scheme and make him consistent. The certain moral scheme is what object to..........you mustn't look in my novel for the old stable ego of the character. There is another ego, according to whose action the individual is

> unrecognizable, and passes through, as it were, allotropic states which it needs a deeper sense than any we've been used to exercise, to discover are states of the same single radically unchanged element.[17]

By "the old stable ago" Lawrence means the "body of accepted consciousness" which one receives from one's father and grandfathers. The ego is, according to him "a sort of second self" which one carries about oneself. In his opinion, the work "ego" implies the sum total of what a man thinks him to be. What a man considers himself to is distinct from his real self—his true and particular nature which cannot be interpreted and analysed precisely, but which can easily be felt and seen in every of his self-consciousness a man makes an image of himself and mostly lives in consonance with that. The real essence of a man always lies beneath superficial self. Lawrence shows it passes through allotropic states which are the states of the same single radically unchanged element. This does not mean that all people are essentially the same. What he means by the "same single radically unchanged element" is "the flame of a man, which burns brighter or dimmer, bluer or yellowier, or redder, rising or sinking or flaring according to the draughts of circumstance and the changing air of life, changing itself continually, yet remaining one single separate, flame, flickering in a strangle world." Lawrence is not satisfied with portraying characters at conventional level. He wants to portray the essence, the fathomless depth of life.

This emphasis, on the inner reality, the reality below consciousness and below will, is also one of the strengths of Lawrence, though at times it also got in his way. For Lawrence is right, there is a dark core of being, there is a flame or a life everlasting, wreathing through the cosmos for ever and giving us our renewal once we can get in touch with it. It is thus, by introducing the unknown dark, forces in action that Lawrence was able to portray his people as they. "humanly physiologically, psychologically, materially" are. And this sense of reality makes Lawrence worth listening to. And for this reason Lawrence, with all his wordiness, his languor, his digressions, is worth listening to.

Lawrence was interested in feelings which are going to carry us through into the next level's therefore, wanted the novel to break a way through, like a hole in the wall, in order to discover a new world outside. Lawrence's own novels embody his vision of life, revealed in terms of man's living revving relationships to his circumambient universe. Through his novels, by exposing the dark corner's of mind, Lawrence wants to bring about a change in the social conditions and create better moral conditions, To achieve his aim Lawrence practices psychoanalysis, In the following chapters all the major novels from The White Peacock to Lady Chatterley's lover—are and individual morality are inextricably interwoven and which portray the essence, the fathomless depth of life and mind.

NOTES AND REFERENCES

1. Yudhistar, *Conflict in the Novels of D. H. Lawrence*, Oliver and Boyd; 1969, p.1.
2. Leon Edel, *The Psychological Novel* (1900-1950), Textbook Publishers, 2003, p. 208
3. Leon Edel, *The Psychological Novel* (1900-1950), Textbook Publishers, 2003. p. 208
4. Phoenix: *The Posthumous Papers of D. H. Lawrence*, The Viking Press, 1936, p. 802.
5. D.H. Lawrence, *The Principles* in Phoneix II, eds Warren Roberts and Harry T. Moore (London: Heinemann, 1968), p. 802.

6. *Ibid.*, p. 173, ISBN 0838907857.
7. *Ibid.*, p. 173. ISBN 0838907857.
8. *Ibid.*, p. 174. ISBN 0838907857.
9. *The Collected Letters II of D.H. Lawrence*, ed., Harry .T. moore (2 vols), Lodon (Heinemann) 1962. II, pp. 826-27.
10. *Studies in Classic American Literature*, Phoenix edition, London, (Heinemann), 1964, p. 76.
11. Yudhistar, *Conflict in the Novels of D. H. Lawrence*, Oliver and Boyd; 1969, pp. 40-47.
12. D.H. Lawrence, *The Principles* in Phoneix II, eds Warren Roberts and Harry T. Moore (London: Heinemann, 1968), p- 477
13. D.H. Lawrence, *The Principles* in Phoneix II, eds Warren Roberts and Harry T. Moore (London: Heinemann, 1968), p. 476.
14. Graham Hough, *The Dark Sun: A Study of D.H. Lawrence* (London:Gerald Duckworth, 1966) pp. 27-28.
15. *The Collected Letters II of D.H. Lawrence*, ed., Harry T. Moore (2vols) Lodon (Heinemann) 1962, pp. 197-198.
16. D.H. Lawrence, *The Principles* in Phoneix II, eds Warren Roberts and Harry T. Moore (London: Heinemann, 1968), p. 71.
17. D.H. Lawrence, *The Principles* in Phoneix II, eds Warren Roberts and Harry T. Moore (London : Heinemann, 1968), p. 380.

3

THE MAJOR NOVELS

I. THE WHITE PEACOCK

Lawrence wrote his first novel *The White Peacock* for six times before it was published in its final form in 1911. He had been tussling away, he tells us, for four years getting it out, "in inchoate bits, from the underground of (my) consciousness" Jessie chambers has recorded how Lawrence told her that he wanted to try writing a novel on the pattern of George Eliot's novels. The usual plan is to take two couples and develop their relationships", he said. "Most of George Eliot's are on that plan. Anyhow I don't want a plot, I should be bored with it. I shall try two couples for a start "[1].

Another thing he told her was that while in the novels of "Fielding and the others the action had been outside; George Eliot started putting all the action inside."[2] He himself wondered which was right and concluded by saying that there ought to be a bit of both. Two or three, things clearly emerge from this. Lawrence, it can be seen, was trying from the very start to go deep into the "underground of [his] consciousness" in order to write fiction. Secondly, he was not interested in any conventional plot as such. In the novel his interest lay in developing the relationships, of his characters, letting the plot take care of itself. Also, he wanted to combine a certain amount of realistic writing with a description of what goes on inside the minds of the characters. His correspondence of the period also reveals how little he cared about the pedantic rules or principles of artistic creation commonly accepted by novelists and critics at the time. Writing in 1908, to Blanche Jennings, discussing his first novel, he said:

> I wish you......to read and criticize some writing of mine that purports to be a novel..... I would not ask you to criticize it so much as a work of art...... applying to it the tests of artistic principles and such like Jargon.... but I would like you to tell me frankly whether it is bright, entertaining and convincing or the reverse.[3]

Lawrence was sure that his novel had "some real good stuff". Even though the narrative was not naturalistic enough to satisfy who only cared about "whether such people could really exist, and live other folk". Lawrence himself was not bothered by this; social realism was not his main aim: "I don't care a damn", he commented, "whether they live or whether they don't,"[4] His purpose was to explore human relationships imaginatively so as to reveal the limitations or failures in them, and also their possibilities.

Lawrence had set out with the idea of taking two couples and working out their relationships. In a way there are two couples whose relations, before and after marriage, seem to have been developed in the course of the novel. Lattie and Leslie, George and Meg. A closer look at the novel, however, reveals that essentially there is only one relationship around which the entire novel moves – that of George and Lattie; and that all other characters and relationships are meant, by way of comparison or contrast, to be direct or indirect comments on this relationship.

Viewed thus, the appearance of the father (Beardsall) and of the gamekeeper (Annable) in the narrative can be seen to be an integral part of the novels design. And their tales no longer remain irrelevant episodes introduced for their own sake, as some have thought. The struggle presented in the novel is struggle for man's wholeness, attained through adequate, satisfactory relationships. The main narrative, reinforced by thematically related episodes, dramatizes how various characters fail to attain wholeness of being through the reconciliation of their basic dual needs.

George, an earth bound young farmer, is shown in the opening pages of the novel to be leading a self-satisfied animal existence. His sister, Emily, who compares him to a fatted calf,[4] thinks he is callous and brutal. Lettie who is fond of him, though also aware of his limitation, refers to him as "My Taurus" and tells him that all he has learnt to like in life is a good dinner, a warm heart, and a lazy evening. But George is at the same time stirring to educate himself. He is fond of reading and through his association with his friend Cyril (the first person narrator of the tale) and Lettie he is awakened to consciousness. Lettie, in the chapter entitled "A vendor of visions" tries to wake him up to another existence by talking to him of music and painting and of death and suffering; not all of which he understands. She tells him, "you are blind; you are only half born; you are gross with good living and heavy sleeping. You are a piano which will only play a dozen common notes. Sunset is nothing to you-it merely happens anywhere. Oh! but make me feel as if I'd like to make you suffer. "His friend with Cyril acquaints him with new subjects-chemistry, botany, psychology. Cyril tells him, while they both work on the farm through the still mornings, of life, of sex and its origins; of Schopenhauer and William James. They talk a great deal of poetry and of metaphysic. George rapidly makes all these ideas part of himself.

In course of time, all this makes him dissatisfied with his existence and he comes to feel "like a toad in a hole." He feels he cannot change because everything around him keeps the same. Living in the same place he feels like a bit of the old building walking, his old feelings sticking to him "like the lichens on the walls." But his problem is not a simple one of moving away from the old place. He rightly dreads what he calls the "slow crumpling away from my foundations," for as soon as his connection with the land is broken, he begins to decay. The process of uprootedness is graphically represented in the novel when George points out to Cyril a sycamore which—even though it keeps on growing is spoiled, its fine balance of leaves gone, because its leading shoot was broken away off when the tree was young. George, when he has broken away from the land, has a similar experience. "I seem thrown off my balance," He tells Cyril. He now feels cut-off from everything, and experiences a sense of loneliness like a vacuum... all loose in the middle of a space of darkness. All connections broken, to decline steadily, he starts drinking hard, until at the end he is completely alienated.

> Like a tree that is falling, going soft and pale and rotten, clammy with small fungi, he stood leaning against the gate, while the dim afternoon drifted with a flow of thick sweet sunshine past him, not touching him.[5]

George's problem has been the complex one of responding to the demands of his awakening consciousness while remaining at the same time rooted in his connection with the soil, of answering the needs both of his spirit and of his flesh. The failure of his relationship with Lettie is in the main attributable to a failure of will in him, a failure to accept the responsibilities of consciousness.

Lattie's constant references to George in the opening

pages of the novel as "bos-bovis; an ox," "a primitive man,"[6] and her remainders to him that he only loves food and comfort and knows practically nothing, are meant to provoke George into taking the initiative and acting for himself. But as soon as he beings to understand and tries to act, Lettie draws back in panic. She admires his "physical beauty, as if were some great firm bud of life,[7] but believes in feminine passivity and, instead of responding to his feelings, expects to be held and kept by him." When George, however, proves slow and Lettie becomes apprehensive that he "would for ever hang fire." She "pulls down the small gold grapes" and chooses a life of comfort and respectability by getting engaged to Leslie. Cyril, too, now tells George. "You should have gripped her before and kept her,"[8] Lettie's explanation to George for her action is that she couldn't help it, that she was expected to act the way she did, "and you're bound to do what people expect you to do."[9] George is, understandably, not satisfied by this piece of reasoning and finds himself in a fix. He feels that Lettie, having started him off, has left him at a loose end, and he blames her for it.

> "You played with me, and showed me heaps of things... you have awakened my life-imagined things that I couldn't have done." In an inspired moment the realization dawns on George that he wants Lettie more than anything, that he must have her, and so decides to ask her to marry him. But even after he has found out that "it doesn't do to go on dreaming," he lingers on and misses his chance of asking Lettie, occasioning Cyrils comment: "He has not asked her, the idiot."[10] Cyril tells George later on that he should have insisted and made his own destiny[11].

When Lettie is married to Leslie, George decides to get married to the "soft and warm" Meg, women of great physical charm. Her love for George is generous. He finds her easy and lovely, "full of soothing and comfort.....trust and lovingness, and he is "incredibly happy"[12] for a time in his amused indulgence of his voluptuous but uneducated wife. This, however, does not last very long. He finds after a few years that he had no longer the peace and quite he used to have while he worked on the farm. He cannot even find time to read. Now "it's the kids all day and the kids all night."[13] Meg finds her fulfillment in the children, performing her role as mother to perfection. George finds himself excluded from all this. "Meg never found any pleasure in me," he remarks bitterly to Cyril. "As she does in the kinds." No wonder that George discovers marriage to be "more of a dual than a duet" in which one party wins and takes the other captive, slave, servant." In the martial duel Meg wins the victory over her husband (as do Emily and Lettie over their husbands) because she has the children on her side.

George had decided to marry Meg because he had "built on Lettie," and when Lettie was gone he was at a dead loss having nothing definite to shape his life to. "I have looked to marriage," he confesses to Cyril, "to set me busy on my house of life, something whole and complete, of which it will supply the design. I must marry or be in a lost lane."[14] Having served himself from his roots in the soil, he dreads "the complete darkness" of his "solitariness," and needs: Lettie, who had made him "conscious", for a light. All that Lettie succeeds in doing, however, is to cause a split in him, graphically represented in the novel by the "fine parting" she makes in his hair. George has been left to choose either vitality or idealism, the life of the senses or that of the spirit, whereas a whole and complete life would have been possible for him only when the needs of both his physical body and his awakened consciousness had been satisfied.

In order to underline the fact that George's problem has no simple and easy solution Lawrence introduces into the narrative the episodes of the father and of the gamekeeper, Annabel. These incidents illustrate the complexity of situations like the one in which George is placed. If George had not been roused to consciousness by Lettie and Cyril, would that have been a satisfactory situation? The answer given by the story of the gamekeeper points out that renouncing deliberately the responsibilities of consciousness is no way out, either.

Answering the criticism that the incident of the father Beardsall was not quite relevant to the narrative, Lawrence wrote to Bianche Jennings: "The father incident is not unnecessary – there is a point, there are heaps of points, I told you there would be, but you have not bothered to find them."[15] The point, however, is not – as Richard Aldington and some others have thought – that Lawrence wanted to express his dislike for his own father in making the father in the novel die of drink. The character of Frank Beardsall is in fact presented with much sympathy and understanding. He is shown to have suffered more than his wife. He saves money and leaves behind as much as four thousand pounds for his wife and children. His wife, when he is dead, realises that she was at fault in having set the children against him while he needed them, just because her "illusion of him", her "romance" was shattered soon after marriage. The death of Frank Beardsall has significance in that it brings a new consciousness to Cyril and Lettie, making them reflect on "the unanswered cry of failure" in the relationship of their parents.

The story of the gamekeeper has been judged to be "entirely irrelevant", "in corporated into the book for no reason at all".[16] But the reason is fairly obvious. Lawrence himself, defending Annables presence in the book is, said to have told Jessie Chambers, "He has to be there. Don't you see why? He makes a sort of balance. Otherwise it's too much one thing, too much me". But there is a more important reason. Annable's life story is an illuminating comment on the possibilities of relationship between George and Lettie. There are many parallels between George and Annable, Lady Crystabel and Lettie. Annable is Lady Crystables animal, "Son animal-son boeuf", Lettie calls George "Bos-bons; an ox". The Lady views Annable "in an aesthetic light" ("I was Greek statues for her", he relates to Curill), — Lettie finds George "Picturesque...... quite fit for a idyll." Lady Crystabel begins "to get souly"; Lettie is also referred to in the novel as one of the "souly sort". Both of them are said to live life at second hand. More than all this it is the peacock symbol which relates Lettie and Lady Crystabel.

One day while Cyril and the gamekeeper are standing in the churchyard, a peacock comes flapping up the terraces and perches on the neck of "an old bowed angel". The bird bends its voluptuous neck, peers about, then lifts up its head and yells.

The sound tore the dark sanctuary of twilight. The old grey grass seemed to stir, and I could fancy the smothered primroses and violets beneath it waking and gasping for fear. The keeper looked at me and smiled. He nodded his head towards the peacock, saying:

> "Hard at that damned thing!"
>
> Again the bird lifted its crested head and gave a cry, at the same time turning awkwardly on its ugly legs, so that it showed us the full wealth of its tail glimmering like a stream of colored stars over the sunken face of the angel. "The proud fool!-look at it! Perched on

> an angle, too, as if it were a pedestal for vanity. That's the soul of a woman or it's the devil."[17]
>
> He was silent for a time, and we watched the great bird moving uneasily before us in the twilight.
>
> "That's the very soul of a lady," he said, "the very, very soul. Damn the thing, to perch on that old angel. I should like to wring its neck."
>
> Again the bird screamed, and shifted awkwardly on its legs....
>
> Annable picks up a piece of sod and flings it at the bird. When the peacock flaps away down the terraces, Annable exclaims, "Just look! The miserable brute has dirtied that angel. A woman to the end, I tell you, all vanity and screech and defilement."

The identification between Lady Crystabel and the peacock is obvious enough in the passage, and when a little later Annabel remarks that it wasn't all Lady Crystabel's fault, and Cyril suggests, "A white peacock, we will say", the gamekeeper laughs and say "yes, she was fair enough." The white in the novels title, as one critic rightly remarks, indicates a moral quality ("spotless"; "without blemish"), but is meant to be pejorative "for the purity suggested by the equivocal adjective is really an avoidance of life".[18] Lettie, too, is guilty of avoiding life (The epithet "white" is used for her frequently. "A White violet, is she?" Cyril says of her) and has a number of peacock characteristics. The parallel is made quite explicit at one point where Lettie's "splendor" is compared to that of a peacock."

> Lettie stood between the firelight and the dusky lamp-glow, tall and warm between the lights. A she turned laughing to the two men, she let her cloak slide over her while shoulder and fall with silk splendor of a peacock's gorgeous blue over the arm of the large

> settee. There she stood with her white hand upon the peacock of her cloak, where it humbled against her dull orange dress. She knew her splendor, and she drew up her throat laughing and brilliant with triumph.[19]

"To be responsible for the good progress of one's life" is indeed the heaviest of responsibilities. No character in the novel succeeds in facing the responsibilities of his or her own development. Not Annable, certainly for he virtually goes back on his development, hating all signs of culture, and holding civilization to be, "the painted fungus of rottenness".[20] He is, as he says himself, "like a good house, built and finished, and left to tumble down again with nobody to live in it".[21] He has come to believe in the motto: "Be a good animal; true to your animal instinct". His advice to all is: Be a good animal, do as the animals do. In the novel, demon", "devil", "devil of the woods", and "Pan" are the words used to refer to him. Another significant association of his is with snowdrops. His appearance "like some malicious pan" just as Lettie is reflecting on how the mysterious: snow drops seem to her "something out of an old religion that we have lost", is not fortuitous. Lettie thinks that the snowdrops "belong to some knowledge we have lost, that I have lost and that I need".[22] What she together with all of us—has lost and needs is what the character of the gamekeeper serves to emphasize in the novel. But the animal like existence of the gamekeeper is, in itself, no more "whole and complete" life than the second hand living of the novels white peacock. Annable is by no means what Graham Hough unwittingly suggests– "the first bearer of the Lawrentian philosophy"[23]; for belief "only in the physical" and scorn for "all spirituality" is no tenet of the Lawrentian creed.

The misery of the man-woman relationship is one of the theme of *The White Peacock*. The male and the female stand for the different values, but they are attracted to each other and they need each other. This gives rise to an unending conflict. Moreover, the barriers of class, education, culture and idealism come in the way of the union. The relationship between men and women remains tragically unbalanced Cyril's own relationship with Emily is a failure, perhaps because they are both inhibited. With some hope he turns to friendship with men, the theme developed in later novels of Lawrence, but in this novel it comes to nothing.

A variety of themes and motives are stirring vaguely in The White Peacock; some are hinted at and dropped, some are partly developed, and almost all reappear in Lawrence's maturer writings. "The White Peacock is like a dream before it is interpreted, or before the possibility of interpretation has been entertained. Many of the classic Laurentian motives which he was later to drag out into consciousness and expand and comment on here appear unanalyzed and unaware of their own significance. We need only to enumerate them briefly: the relationship with Jessie Chambers, to be elaborated and finally exercised in *Sons and Lovers*; the hostility to the father, and hence to the principle of authority in general, the conflict for a woman between a self-conscious, civilized man and an earth-bound, in articulate one; the degeneration of the man who denies his own potentialities; the gamekeeper, with his violent hatred of modern women and their standards; the lady who gives herself to a more primitive kind of man; the love-relation between man and man, almost overtly homosexual in the "Poem of Friendship" chapter of The *White Peacock*, later concealed and distorted in *Women in Love*, Aaron's Rod, Kangaroo and *The Plumed Serpent*.

There is enough here for a dozen stories, and they were duly written later on. Their co-presence in *The*

> *White Peacock* suggests a certain confusion of purpose. But although Lawrence is bursting with all this rich stock of material, he knows quite enough about conventional novel structure to subordinate most of it to a single central plot the story of Lettic and her two Suitors.[24]

The *White Peacock* is hardly worth attention as a novel in its own right. "Ford Moddore Hueffer, Lawrence's first literary advisor, said "it's got every fault the English novel can have." But he added "you've got genius;"[25] For Hueffer recognized the authentic eye, the fine sensibility, the original handling of distinctive themes, most of all the life that runs through even the most cloying prose – qualities not altogether cancelled out by immaturity and formlessness. The very evasions and desperate measures are significant; we can trace the problems Lawrence, had to face, and the solutions he came through to, before he could render his own deepest experience into art with the poise and assurance of Sons and Lovers.

> *The White Peacock* is certainly Lawrence's amateurish work. Even an ardent admirer of D.H. Lawrence, F.R. Leavis, says of it as "Painfully Callow". Lawrence himself was aware of its weaknesses. Writing to Blanche Jennings whom he had submitted the first version of the novel, he says, "I shrink from the thought of any one reading that work – if I were not vain and poor I should like to put it in the fire."[26]

The White Peacock leads one to wonder what would have become of Lawrence the novelist if he had not found it necessary also to become a prophet. Most of his later themes and ideas are found here in something more than embryonic for. But they have not yet become articles of faith. Leaving aside some youthful immaturities *The White Peacock* has a singularly pure and untrammeled kind of discernment. But his pure vision is not enough for Lawrence; the impulse to theorise and expand on what he had seen was always strong in him, and having achieved what he could with the candid gaze of his youth, he immediately gives it up, in pursuit of something more turbid and more difficult."[27]

The White Peacock, on the whole, is not a successful novel. The impression it leaves on the reader is a very diffuse one. It is more a generalized statement than a working out of the conflicts latent in the relationship it deals with tentatively. Most of the themes and conflicts vaguely suggested here were developed and powerfully presented by Lawrence in his subsequent novels. Neither his vision nor his style has yet the sharpness and intensity which are the distinctive features of his later novels. But as his very first novel, it establishes the moral intentions of Lawrence. The very title "The White Peacock" indicates a moral quality ("Spotless"; "without blemish") it is also clear from the novel that Lawrence's concern in his novels is "the imaginative explorations of life in its various relationships."

II. SONS AND LOVERS

> "There is probably no phrase much more hackneyed than that of 'human document'. Yet it is the only one which at all describes this very unusual book. It is hardly a story: rather the first part of a man's life, from his birth until his twenty-fifth year, the conditions surrounding him, his strength and his numerous weaknesses. Put before us in a manner, which misses no subtlest effect either of emotion or environment. And the heroine of the book is not sweet heart, but mother the mother with whose marriage the novel begins, with whose pathetic death it reaches its climax. The love for each other of the mother and her son,

> Paul Morel, is the mainspring of both their lives; it is portrayed tenderly, yet with a truthfulness which slurs nothing even of that friction which is unavoidable between the members of two different generations."[28]

In Sons and Lovers there is much more immediacy, realization, than in the callow and conventional earlier novels. Lawrence himself describes the treatment as 'visualised' – "in that hard, violent style full of sensation and presentation. "Paul Morel will be a novel – not a florid prose poem, or a decorated idyll running to seed in realism."[29] The autobiographical and intensely personal subject matter contributes much in these terms. Here Mr. Lawrence has found the very core of himself; here he has dipped deep into his own childhood, setting down all that he ever knew or felt. We notice a sudden exquisite refinement of psychological texture, a new, painstaking reverence for the most subtle and intangible details of motivation. The problem of miss-mating is no longer studied in an already established marital relation; here it is not a matter of miss-mating at all but of a radical inability to mate. This inability of Mr. Lawrence seeks to explain entirely in terms of his hero's emotional relation to his parents.

That is the really new and contributive thing about Sons and Lovers. Paul Morel's childhood unfolds in the vitiated atmosphere of an already unhappy marriage. In the married life of the Morels Mr. Lawrence gives us a miss-mating which both he and we thoroughly understand. The marriage of this drunken, bullying, morally weak-fibred miner to a woman of superior breeding and a stern, sensitive, puritanically ingenuous temperament, was fore doomed to failure. Her hatred and aversion for him is absorbed by her child almost from the cradle, so that at the age of six Paul prays that his father may be killed. Cut-off from companionship with his father – and there can be no doubt that a child learns to love the father largely through imitating its mother – Paul abnormally concentrates all his affection upon one parent.

Under the strain of these relations the boy develops a premature emotional maturity. His childish heart is torn between anguish for his abused mother and a scarcely repressed hatred for his brutal father. Mrs. Morel, her affection for her husband completely atrophied, now turns altogether to her son and deliberately courts his allegiance. He becomes her confidant and her consoler, a quiet, worldly wise child whose natural initiative is gradually deadened by the burden of this unequal responsibility, while at the same time the too great absorption in his mother effeminizes him. At a time when most children already display the first poetic tentative of the mating impulse in ideal comradeships with playmates of the opposite sex, Paul dreams only of running away with his mother and living alone with her for the rest of his life.

By the time Paul reaches adolescence the distortion is already complete. He finds himself attracted to Miriam Leviers, a shy, beautiful girl who idealizes him. But the prospect of marrying her fills him only with unhappiness and a strange, paralyzing sense of death. The author now boldly underlines the mutual infatuation of mother and son. A jealous conflict, in which Paul is the helpless pawn, ensures between the two women Paul gradually becomes persuaded of the unreality of his and Miriam's feelings; and returns to his exultant mother with the tragic conviction that while she is alive no other woman can have place in his affections. There is a final flaring up of his mating impulse towards Clara Dowse, a married woman of strong, sensuous appeal. While under her influence he returns to Miriam and finally possesses both women, hovering for a time between what are for him the sacred and profane loves of his life. His consciousness that with Clara he is merely indulging in a temporary liaison with a married woman makes it easier for him to give himself to her. But in the end Mrs. Morel triumphs again and brings Paul to her death – bed, a confessed and repentant lover. Her death, now desired and even criminally hastened by him as an emancipation from an intolerable situation, makes her triumph only the more complete and leaves Paul standing before us a helpless, tragic, pathetically childish figure. In a final unforgettable chapter Mr. Lawrence pictures him as a human derelict set adrift, with the great nostalgia for death in his hearts, and living merely in the memory of a relation which, hallowed only in childhood, has grown utterly ruinous in its perpetuations.

No summary can convey the pathos of *Sons and Lovers*. With all its power and its passion, it remains to a certain extent incomprehensible. We may, for the moment, accept it intuitively. But we hesitate to accept it in its implications. The very idea that an excess of mother love should prove so disastrous to an individual's fate seems monstrous. Instinctively we look upon this as an exceptional case, and fortify ourselves against it by calling the book morbid or perverse. But at the same time we can never fully discard the element of truth eminent in the novel. Freud has proved beyond cavil that the parental influence regularly determines the mating impulse. The child's attachment to the parent of opposite sex becomes the prototype of all later Love relations. In the normal development, this first infatuation is gradually obliterated from memory by widening associations and by transference, but any disturbance in the balanced and harmonious influence of both parents upon the child, or any abnormal pressure of circumstances or willful action that forces the child into a specialized attitude towards either parent subtly effects the later love life of the child. With the aid of the Freudian theory we begin to see in Paul, the tremendous role that the abnormal fixation upon the parent (mother) plays in the psychic development of the individual. And thus we approach the novel with a greater understanding:

> Why has the attitude of the son to his mother here had such a devastating effect upon his whole life; why could he not overcome this obstacle like other children and ultimately attain some measure of manhood? Why, in short, was the surrender so complete? In Paul's case the abnormal fixation upon the mother is most obviously conditioned by the father, whose unnatural position in the family is responsible for the distortion of the normal attitude of the child towards its parents. The father ideal simply does not exist for Paul; where there should have been an attractive standard of masculinity to imitate, he can only fear and despise. The child's normal dependence upon the mother is perpetuated because there is no counter-influence to detach it from her. But there is another distortion, equally obvious, which fatally influences the natural development. Paul's early fixation upon his mother is met and enhanced by Mrs. Morel's abnormally concentrated affection for her son. Her unappeased love, which can no longer go out towards her husband, turns to Paul for consolation; she makes him love her too well. Her love becomes a veritable Pandora's Box of evil. For Paul is now hemmed in on all sides by too much love and too much hate.[30]

Lawrence himself in a letter to Edward Garnett (14th November 1912) has expressed similar opinion about the novel. While discussing the theme or central idea of the novel:

> It follows this idea: a woman of character and refinement goes into the lower class, and has no satisfaction in her own life. She has had a passion

> for her husband, so the children are born of passion and have heaps of vitality. But as her sons grow up. She selects them as lovers – first the eldest, then the second. These sons are urged into life by their reciprocal love of their mother – urged on and on. But when they come to manhood, they can't love, because their mother is the strongest power in their lives, and holds them......As soon as the young men come into contact with women, there's a split. William gives his sex to a fribble, and his mother holds his soul. But the split kills him, because he doesn't know where he is. The next son gets a woman who fights for his soul – fights his mother. The son loves the mother – all the sons hate and are jealous of the father. The battle goes on between the mother and the girl, with the son as object. The mother gradually proves stronger, because of the tie of blood. The son decides to leave his soul in his mother's hands, and, like his elder brother go for passion. He gets passion. Then the split begins to tell again. But, almost unconsciously, the mother realizes what the matter is, and begins to die. He is left in the end naked of everything, with the drift towards death.......Now tell me if I haven't worked out my theme, like life, but always my theme..... if you can't see the development – which is slow, like growth – I can.[31]

Sons and Lowers, however, is not a novel about the Oedipus complex or mother fixation of the Freadians. Lawrence had heard of Freud before he wrote the final draft of the novel, but he never subscribed to any theories of Freudianism – which he took to be a branch of medical science, interesting in many respects, but quite often wrong and limited in its approach. Referring to one of the reviews of *Sons and Lovers*, published in a Journal of Psycho-analysis, Lawrence remarked in a letter to Barbara Low:

> You know I think 'complexes' are vicious half statements of the Freudians: sort of can't see wood for trees. When you've said Mutter– complex, you've said nothing - ......, a complex is not simply a sex relation: far from it – My poor book: it was, as art, a fairly complete truth: so they carve a half lie out of it, and say "Volia' Swine.[32]

Lawrence's protest was against distortion of the total meaning of his novel. "Father complex, mother complex, incest dreams: pah, when we've had the little excitement out of them we shall forget them as we have forgotten so many other catch-words", he wrote later in Fantasia. But he was not unaware of the element of truth in the findings of psychoanalysis. He recognized, and stressed, that even a relation of intense pure sympathy or sacred love between parent and child "inevitably involves us in a conclusion of incest" – though to distinguish his views from those of the Freudians he calls it "spiritual incest", which he nevertheless describes as even more dangerous than sensual incest because it is less instinctively repugnant. Lawrence had written in his forward to Sons and Lovers that it is in the Flesh, in Woman, that we have our knowledge of god, the Father, the unknowable. "In her we go back to the Father.......blind and unconscious. "Every woman demands that her man, having done his day's work should come to her with joy and be renewed, "be re-born of her", so that he can go forth again the next morning with his new strength."[33]

> But if the man does not come home to a woman ... to be warmed, and restored and nourished, ... Then she shall expel him from the house .... For in the flesh of the woman does God exact Himself. And out of the flesh of the woman does. He demand: "Carry this of Me forth to utterance". And if the man deny,

> or be too weak, then shall the woman find another man, of greater strength. And if, because of the word, which is the law, she do not find another man, nor he another woman, then shall they both be destroyed. For he, to get that rest, and warmth, and nourishment which he should have had from her, his woman, must consume his own flesh, and so destroy himself, whether with wine, or other kindling. And she, either her surplus shall wear away her flesh, in sickness, or in lighting up and illuminating old dead words, or shall spend it in fighting with her man to make him take her, or she shall turn to her son, and say 'Be you my Go-between'[34].
>
> But the man who is the go-between from woman to production is the lover of that woman. And if that woman be his mother, then is he her lover in part only; he carries for her, but is never received into her for his confirmation and renewal, and so wastes himself away in the flesh. The old son-lover was Oedipus. The name of the new one is legion. And if a son lover take a wife, then is she not his wife, she is only his bed. And his life will be torn in twain, and his wife in her despair shall hope for sons, that she may have her lover in her hour.[35]

These views are further elaborated in Fantasia, where Lawrence explains how an exaggerated and intense spiritual love from the parent's leads to a painfully false relation between parents and children. By establishing a dynamic relation with the child in the second plane of consciousness, the parents – because of their monomania for love and more love – do "what is vicious for any parent to do" Parents, instead of helping the child's growth into manhood so that he would in his time. "possess his own soul in strength within him, deep and alone", make it impossible for him to grow. When a woman has attained her fulfillment through love, deep sensual love, and exquisite sensitive communion", she should make the great resolution to come to rest within herself, living in peace and equilibrium with her husband. Instead, her craving for more love makes her look round for a new sort of lover, one who will "understand" her; and as often as not she turns to her son. In him she provokes what she wants.

He is a medium to her, she provokes form him her own answer. So she throws herself into a last great love for her son, a final and fatal devotion, that which would have been the richness and strength of her husband and is prison to the boy.

The intense non-sexual parent – child love has fore stalled the great love experience which should lie in the future. "The cream is licked off from life before the boy or the girl is twenty. Afterwards – repetition, disillusion, and barrenness"

Sons and Lovers presents this argument dramatically in a most effective and convincing manner. It impresses on the reader the long term risks involved in too intimate – even if no libidinous – family relationships which appear to flourish so very well in the short run. If such a relationship as Mrs. Morel's with Paul only prevents the son from finding proper fulfillment in life, then – the novel suggests – we most look closely into our ideas about parent child relationship in order to ensure that every child has the opportunity of a free and full development.

The sections of the novel which deal with Paul's love affairs with Miriam and Clara depict the success and the failures, the harmonies and the conflicts in the relationships with remarkable accuracy and power. It must also be said that the achievement of Sons and Lovers in this part of the book is overshadowed by Lawrence's far more brilliant and outstanding achievement in his next two novel's – *The Rainbow* and *Women in Love* – where he draws with a rare beauty and incomparable power possibly the best imaginatively realized picture in the English language of the conflict-ridden relations between men and women in search of a satisfying, harmonious, and meaningful life together.

III. THE RAINBOW

> Manners and morals: they are, critics agree, what novels properly concern themselves with; and the specialists in the English novel can readily demonstrate the English novelist expert attention to both from Moll Flanders to greatest thriller by Graham Greene. Certainly, fiction is of all literacy genres the most intractable to description or definition, and we are grateful for any indices to its nature.... Even Dr. Leavis, who demotes or dismisses Richardson, Fielding, Sterne, Smollett, Dickens, Thakeray, Hardy and Joyce, expresses much admiration for Hawthorne, and finds a great tradition in Jane Austen, George Eliot, James Conrad, and Lawrence, in whose work, as it seems to him, manners are so chosen and placed as to reflect on their particular surfaces the image of that sober absolute morality, essentially secular and embattled, which for two centuries has been the strength of England if not of the entire civilized world.[36]

Whether the English novelist is examining, with intelligence or sentimentality or cynicism, the manners and squeamishness of the cultivated provinces or the local colour of urban and rural low life, or the sinister fascinations of the haut monde, or the convulsive freakishness of grand super sexual and asexual passions, or the palpitating idealism of young women who – not having been told what they can importantly do – are looking for something important to do. Whatever the English Novelist tries the manners and morals of the earliest and most oppressively successful middle class, in history are breathing down his neck and directing his pen into the official view of a life that is in any case considerably less exhilarating than the life visible to the great continental novelists. Or, for that matter, to Chaucer and Shakespeare.

The bourgeois imperative which has defended the materialist order against its gravest threat, and which Anglo-Saxon fiction had perforce to accept for two centuries is the imperative against human normality. You men, the imperative declares, transcend sex by the rhetoric of a grand passion, you may cheapen it as by Fielding's characteristic resort to comic strip prurience, you may ignore it or Jeer at it, you may even in extremity be clinical about it, but you may not regard it as a serious, normal, central preoccupation of mankind, and you may not attempt to understand it.

The first literary effect of such a proscription was to deprive English fiction of normal women. The sphere of decision of women, in Western civilization has always been love and marriage; and if the woman is not permitted to take into account the most serious impulse of her private existence, she may surrender to domesticity or the vapors and become one of Dicken's brave. Biddys or Dumb Doras, or she may be encouraged to transcend sex before going to the trouble of learning what it is, like George Eliot's Dorothea, or Emily Bronte's Cathy or any other Gothic or Romantic heroine...... The English hero, true, has always been allowed some scope of heroic action in adventure (often commercial), in working his way up in "becoming a success".

Still, to eradicate half the human race, and to confine

the energies of the other half mainly within the bound of materialistic aspiration – this is not to survey, through morals and manners, the limits of human possibility. It was this order of things that D.H. Lawrence confronted when he began writing the novel the first part of which eventually became The Rainbow. *The Rainbow* confidently bases itself on the assumption that sex is a serious, normal central preoccupation of mankind. It assumes not only that generations are generated, but that the relationship between husband and wife is the central fact of human existence, that the living nucleus of this relationship is the act of sexual union, that the act of sexual union is infinitely serious, complex and difficult, and that an act of such radiant significance must be fairly treated by the honest novelist. The revolutionary nature of The Rainbow is, then, twofold: it is the first English novel to record the normality and significance of physical passion; and it is the only English novel to record with a prophetic awareness of consequences, the social revolution whereby Western man lost his sense of community and men – more especially, women learned, if they could, that there is no help any longer except in the individual and in his capacity for a passional life.

Lawrence's individuals are different and distinct from one another except when a strength of sympathy draws them together for moments out of the reciprocal alienations of individuality, and every relationship in The Rainbow testifies, not how easy and renewable, but how hard to come by, how precarious, and how irrecoverably unique each instance of passion is, even in a nature as faithful to itself and as sensitively patient as Tom Brongwen's:

..................Then she said:

"You will be good to me, won't you?"

She was small and girlish and terrible, with a queer, wide look in her eyes. His heart leaped in him, in anguish of love and desire, he went blindly to her and took her in his arms. "I want to," he said as he drew her closer and closer in. She was soothed by the stress of his embrace, and remained quite still, relaxed against him, mingling into him. And he let himself go from past and future, was reduced to the moment with her. In which he took her and was with her and there was nothing beyond, they were together in an elemental embrace beyond their superficial foreignness. But in the morning he was uneasy again. She was still foreign and unknown to him. Only, within the fear was pride, belief in him as mate for her. And she, everything forgotten in her new hour of coming to life, radiated vigour and joy. So that he quivered to touch her.

It made a great difference to him, marriage. Things became remote and of so little significance, as he knew the powerful source of his life, eye opened on a new universe, and he wondered in thinking of his triviality before ..... And each time he returned home, he went steadily – expectantly, like a man who goes to a profound, unknown satisfaction ....
He realized that he lived by her. Did he own her? Was she her forever? Or might she go away? She was not really his, it was not a real marriage, this marriage between them. She might go away. He did not feel like a master, husband, father of her children. She belonged elsewhere. Any moment, she might be gone.............And he was ever drawn to her ....he could never quite be satisfied, never be at peace because she might go away........... She was consciously self – sufficient and did not say very much. Occasionally she lifted her head, her grey eyes shining with a

> strange light, that had nothing to do with him, or with this place, and would tell him about herself. She seemed to be back again in the past, chiefly in her childhood or her girlhood, with her father. She very rarely talked of her first husband.[37]

Tom Brangwen's apprehensions are not, after all, merely the customary timeless ones of husbands, but unprecedented seismic shocks. The Rainbow is recording a community in its last flare of vitality and gradual dying away, and all relationships and feelings are shaken by the great change.

The foreignness of Tom's wife represents, disturbingly enough, the essential distance between all men and especially between the sexes; but it is already a terrifying difference beyond natural difference. Tom is no simple farmer, his aspiration toward the irreducibly alien woman is an inarticulate but not unconscious aspiration toward the experience of a life beyond the receding satisfaction of a community in process of dissolution. Until he meets Lydia he refuses, in drink and solitude, the only life his community offers him. Now, his dissatisfactions are new, and the brave chances he takes are new.

Individual aspiration, once it is realized, has no certain or obvious goal; and how can it be held in check somewhere, how can one keep it from making all action or repose seem premature and insufficient, how can the skeptical analytic mind be quieted? In fact, even for Tom these questions have force, the speechless remoteness of his marriage – for all of its passion – is finally not enough, his pathetic paternal jealousy of his step daughter's choice of husband poisons even as it recalls to him his sense of his own life What was missing in his life, that, in his ravening soul, he was not satisfied? He had that friend at school, his mother, his wife and Anna? What had he done? He had failed with his friend, he had been a poor son; but he had known satisfaction with his wife, let it be enough; he loathed himself for the state he was in over Anna. Yet he was not satisfied. It was agony to know it and he was ashamed. He trampled himself to extinguish himself.

So Tom Brangwen dies, drunk as Noah to forget the wearying puzzles of his middle age, drowned in the flood of rain, and his women mourn him: "I shared life with you, I belong in my own way to eternity," said Lydia Brangwen, her heart cold, knowing her own singleness.

This is *Everyman*, not at all the conventional individualist hero of English fiction; and Lawrence, anticipating perplexity, provided his critics with a long peg on which to hang their theories about *The Rainbow* and *Women in Love*. "You mustn't look," he wrote to Edward Garnett who had been disappointed to find no trace of Sons and Lovers in the new work, ".....for the old stable ego of the character. There is another ego, according to whose action the individual is unrecognizable, and passes through, as it were, allotropic states which it needs a deeper sense than any other we've been used to exercise, to discover are states of the same single radically unchanged element."[38]

The trouble is that, in this formulation, Lawrence does not yet seem to have made clear to himself why the old mode of characterization is being discarded and how the new mode functions, and what sort of novel employs one or the other. Sons and Lovers is – like *A Portrait of the Artist* as a *Young Man* – a willful and confused Post Victorian novel of youthful longing and self-discovery, written by a young man whose party rejects or ignores the values of the community which has helped to make him. *The Rainbow,* on the other hand, is an elegiac novel about the dissolution of a community where values, even as these pass away, the author neither rejects nor ignores but seeks to understand and somehow, for his characters, sake, to transcend. The characters (Mr. Morel excepted) in *Sons and Lovers* are Post-Victorian individualists colliding with an angry young individualist of a hero; the characters in *The Rainbow* breath and move, as long as they can, in the large atmosphere of a community. Not that Tom Brangwen is less individual than, say, Paul Morel; a quite contrary, he is more honestly and totally imagined, and therefore more human and more of a man.

What is revolutionary in *The Rainbow* – what makes Lawrence, in perhaps the most important sense, the only modern novelist – is not the mode of characterization, but the new awareness which finds this mode necessary: the awareness that with the dying away, in the ego of technology, of genuine communal relations between men, with the inevitable thwarting of what Lawrence was later to call "the societal impulse", the only hope for man lies in those remaining potentialities of human relationship which depend for their realization on the fullest (not necessarily the most various or complicated) possible realization of the sexual impulse. For Lawrence, then, the hope – in fact the last resort – of modern man is the unhappy word stares at us as it did at Lawrence's censors – Sex: not as cold appetite, not as self – imposed exile from the teeming world, not as the exploiting of sensation or the temporary allaying of an itch, but as the bond of tranquility and faith between man and woman, those polar opponents, and the last renewable proof of human community.

'The Rainbow' is mid passage and arrival. Tom Brangwen still has roots, connections, and the virtue of quietness in solitude; of these vestiges of community Anna and will still keep something by, as it were, barely remembering them, Anna in her slovenly cheerful maternity.

Will in his mute satisfaction with manual labor or minor artisanship. Only Ursula – modern woman and therefore, in her unforeseen and disastrously unprepared for homelessness, true representative of modern mankind – has nothing at all of what, outside themselves, sustained the two generations before her. And for all three generations the unmapped territory to be explored, with increasing desperation and hope, is sex.

Tom Brangwen has a real marriage and his life is transfigured by the reality of passion. If his marriage fails to give him everything, it nevertheless gives him much, even enough to make him at length unhappily sensitive to the unknown vilorations of what he must do without.

For Anna and Will, on the other hand, marriage seems at first sunnier and more simple. They have moved very far out of the shadow of the old Brangwan world, Anna, at least, is impatient with established sanctities; and both of them rejoice on their prolonged honeymoon in an uninhibited mutual exploration of sexuality; day after day of vital time dissolving case:

> As they lay close together ...... lay still, in each other's arms; for their moment they were at the heart of eternity, whilst time rooted far off, forever off, towards the rim. .... Gradually they began to wake up, the noises outside became more real. They understood and answered the call outside. They counted the strokes of the bell. And when they counted midday, they understood that it was midday, in the world, and for themselves also.
>
> It dawned upon her that she was hungry............... And then, quite calmly, even a little surprised, she was in the present, and was saying: "I am dying with hunger".

"So, am I", he said calmly, as if it were of not the slightest significance. And they relapsed into the warm, golden stillness. And the minutes flowed unheeded past the window outside. Then suddenly she stirred against him. "My dear, I am dying of hunger", she said. It was a slight pain to him to be brought to. "We'll get up", he said, unmoving. And she sank her head on to him again, and they lay still, Lapsing........

"Do get up", she murmured at length, "and give me something to eat".

"Yes," he said, and he put his arms round her, and she lay with her face on him. They were faintly astonished that they did not move. In such moments as Lawrence here presents, there can be no "characters" in the conventional fictional sense, The mode of characterization is dictated by the focus of attention, which here is on a core of impulse anterior to personality. Nobody, it is true, can live indefinitely at such a depth of impulse; and the comic ascension of Anna and Will to the level of a more mundane appetite testifies not only to the existence of a daylight world in which we are all, more or less, scrupulously differentiated fictional characters, but also to that respect for full human truth which disciplines even the most rhapsodic utterances in this novel. The careful reader never forgets that The Rainbow is, in one large and traditional aspect, a great realistic novels. Tom Brangwan's life outside marriage, for example, is registered with an immediacy and resonance that would establish him as one of the great figures in English fiction even if he were nothing more; and one thinks of such superb set-pieces as Tom's efforts at comforting the child Anna while Lydia is bearing his first child, Tom's drunkenly inspired eulogy of marriage,

> his death in the flood – a luminous pertinence of detail, a fidelity to locate, a sternness of pathos not readily matched in any other fiction. Nevertheless, as the rhythm of the style always near, when not actually, the rhythm of rhapsodic utterance – persists in implying, life is renewable only and perpetually at the springs of impulse, in celebration and praise, where we are less unique than human; and only to the degree to which we have renewed ourselves there, can we breathe and move as individuals in the daylight world.[39]

Renewal, the gift and aim of life, becomes in modern marriage less and less the gift of repose, more and more pressingly the aim of conscious and personal exploration: woman is less passive and man more anxious, approaching an uneasy identity of roles. Lydia is still withdrawn and enigmatic, a woman of the old dispensation, unhurried, immured in domesticity and unamenable to self questioning; so Tom is the explorer – joyous or baffled in this first marriage, moving doubtfully at the rim of awareness. Anna, on the other hand, has come awake, because the invasion of all things by mechanism and the conscious mind has made Lydia the last possible woman of her kind: having lost what her mother unquestionably had, Anna must make up for it by becoming explorative in her own right, the free companion of her husband. The temperamental differences between Lydia and Tom were unbridgeable, and of no significance to Lydia. Yet wills soft inarticulateness drives the skeptical articulate Anna wild, and Anna's attacks on her husband's temperament drive him into retaliatory fury:

> She.............. clung to the worship of human knowledge. Man must die in the body out in his knowledge he was immortal. Such, somewhere, was her belief, quite obscure and unformulated. She believed I the

> omnipotence of the human mind.

He, on the other hand, blind as a subterranean thing, just ignored the human mind and ran after his own dark-souled desires, following his own tunneling nose, She felt often she must suffocate. And she fought him off.

> Then he, knowing he was blind, fought madly back again, frantic in sensual fear............. "You've a right to do as I want," he cried. "Fool!" she answered. "Fool!"[40]

In the perilous colloidal tension of modern marriage, too much depends on merely personal qualities. And at least for persons living in the delusive afterglow of the old world, still un alert to the swarming problems of consciousness– too much depends on the increasingly elaborate and conscious satisfactions of sexuality: the man, having lost his inherited mastery, comes to depend on these as on a drug, and the woman come to resent what she will eventually regard as his infantile male weakness: Ann and Will near reclaim their honeymoon fulfillment of passion or seem capable of the reconciliation between passion and sensuality, and their lives dwindle away in subtle disorganization, in the minor consummations and complaints of Anna's role as the fecund housewife and Will's as a wood work teacher for the town, "very happy and keen in his new public spirit". Since their imperfect truce is the first modern marriage, it is appropriate that they bring into being the first complete modern woman, totally dispossessed and therefore totally explorative. The child Ursula still has her father's environing and sometimes overpowering love; and she has, also, in conversation with her grandmother, a window on the certainties of the past even as the thought of growing up without such certainties begin to trouble her.

> ....Ursula asked her deepest childish questions of her grandmother. "Will somebody love me grandmother?"
>
> "Many people love you, child, we all love you". "But when I am grown up, will somebody love me?" "Yes, some man will love you, child, because it's your nature. And I hope it will be somebody who will love you for what you are, and not for what he wants of you. But we have a right to want what we want".
>
> Ursula was frightened, hearing these things. Her heart sank; she felt she had no ground under her feet. She clung to her grand mother. Here was peace and security.[41]

Lydia's wisdom in old age is wasted on her granddaughter, and reverberates outward into the large implications of the novel. One of the dangers of marriage in the time of a breaking of bonds is, as Lydia suggests, that a man may be driven to seek in a mate not a distinct and different person as generous and needy as himself, but only what will compensate him, somehow, for his sense of loss – though, tragically, he must have both in order to have either. The marriage of Anna and Will is, at last, a deadlock because neither wife nor husband has the generosity and wisdom to acknowledge and accept the unbreakable different ness of the other; and Tom's response to Lydia's strangeness – at the beginning so compelling an attraction for him – is, at last, to drift back into confusion and the oblivion of drink. Moreover, the grandmother's words to the child Ursula are a prophecy; for Skrebensky will desperately seek in Ursula (as Will sought in Anna) only what might make up for his unmanning sense of loss, and Ursula herself will not understand, not at least till very late, that her promiscuity with Skrebensky is no generous gift of love but only a confession of mutual weakness, no passionate resolution but an increasingly unsatisfactory escape into sex from the unprecedented problems of the modern consciousness.

Still *The Rainbow* is, finally, not about consummation but about promise. *The Rainbow* that Ursula sees at the very end of the novel need not be dismissed as a despairing symbolic stroke to allow a nominal conclusion and to release Lawrence for Women in Love, though the two novels are obviously related in ways more important than the continuance of several characters through the second, it may be that those readers who find the end of *The Rainbow* wanting have turned their minds prematurely to the next book, and expecting what it is not in the theme of the earlier novel to give. No doubt Lawrence's original intention was to write a single novel which would encompass and illustrate in the lives of a family the great social and psychological changes of our century, and which would conclude with a treatment of such individual problems and individual solutions as, indeed, are treated in Women in Love. But it must have come eventually to him that the break down of community was a subject in itself, and that it calumniated appropriately in the coming to consciousness of emancipated, modern woman. If Lawrence had ended the novel with modern woman numbed in her grimace of freedom, he would have been merely cynical; if he had ended with Ursula still unsure of her feelings for Skreben sky, the novel would trail of in a puzzle. The novel does, in fact, end as Ursula, having freed herself of her struggle with Skrebensky, is for the first time genuinely free not only of the un revivable past but of those false ties she has tentatively accepted in place of it. To require any more at least schematically– is to require an unequivocal happy ending, and even in Women in Love or Lady Chatterley's Lover, Lawrence is not that obliging.

The pledge of the future is Ursula's knowledge of what is terrible about the present, and her knowledge derives from a power of passion which must at length be consummated because it would otherwise have had no cause to spring into being. Dostoevsky called the Russians the "god-bearing" people, those who carry the secret of life within them and preserve it for that remote apocalypse when the entire world will be fit to receive it. At the conclusion of *The Rainbow* Ursula is the single god-bearing person left in the world. It is a tribute to the prodigious optimism and persuasiveness of Lawrence's vision that the secret she holds seems worth the keeping until the world is fit to receive it.

IV. WOMEN IN LOVE

'Women in Love' is widely accepted, now, as what F.R. Leavis showed it to be: the major work of a major novelist. And its more recent critics have largely agreed not only on its merits but also on its faults. In their view Lawrence failed to resolve problems he believed that he was resolving or at least set out to resolve and following from this supposed failure of thought they see a failure of structure. Dr. Leavis's statement of the case remains the clearest, 'The diagnosis represented by Gerald and Gudrun is convincing – terribly so, but Birkin and Ursula as a norm, contemplated in the situation they are left in at the close of the book, leaves us wondering (and, it must in fairness be added leave Lawrence wondering too). That is, if certain symmetry of negative and positive was aimed at in Women in Love, Lawrence has been defeated by the difficulty in life. He hasn't solved the problems of civilization that he analyses.'

This criticism, which has been repeated by critics as different as Elisco Vivas and W.W. Robson, rests on some questionable assumptions. One is that Lawrence's intention in the novel can be known apart from, and used as a measure of, his achievement. Another is that the novel is constructed on a simple pattern of contrast – symmetry of negative and positive – between the complete failure of one love affair and the assured success of the other.

A third is that an adequate criticism of any novel can approach it as an analysis of the problems of civilization, to be judged by whether, on a simple practical level, it offers a viable solution.

Lawrence's intentions in writing Women in Love, whatever they may have been, are beside the point. The tale, if we trust it, simply does not present the marriage of Birkin and Ursula as ideal in itself or as an adequate solution to the problems presented. On the contrary an important thesis of the novel is that no fully satisfying personal relationship is possible to people placed, like Birkin and Ursula, in a social and religious vacuum. Lawrence's treatment of their marriage is firmer and less positive, shows a keener awareness of life's difficulties, than any attempt to set up a norm could offer. It follows from this that the structure of the novel must be less symmetrical and more complex than has been supposed. Brikin and Gerald, in particular, are not so diagrammatically opposed. Their destinies do not represent the assured positive solution and a disastrous deviation from it, but something far less definite: a contrast of attitudes, hope against despair, and struggle against surrender.

The subtle structure, the novel actually evolves in not making just that false simplification its critics have thought to see in it may be brought out better by attention to the form rather than the ostensible meaning of the two love stories. The Gerald Gudrun story is closed; it forms a complete action in the Aristotelian sense. The Birkin –

Ursula story is open. It has a beginning and a development, but no end either displayed or implied. The future of his story is not predetermined, and the agents move out of the last pages into the freedom of continued unpredictable endeavor. Looking back over the novel from the clear and conscious inclusiveness of the final paragraph, we can see that this freedom, this making of choices in a continual process of self-commitment, has characterized this couple at every stage of the story. Gerald on the other hand is fated. His doom is fixed from the start, and he abandons himself to the remorseless forces which carry him to it. These forces act as much from within himself as from without, but still he cannot be said to choose his direction. He acquiesces in it, let's himself go; and, paradoxically, this passivity towards his fate, towards the forces of destruction within himself, takes the form of an exertion of the will. Gudrun is caught up in the same processes, and although she does, not literally die her future course too has, by the end of the novel, been rigidly and terrifyingly predetermined. This contrast of form between the two stories leads to a more satisfying evaluation of the novel than the usual way of judging it on what it offers of social diagnosis and therapy. I do not mean that Women in Love is not concerned very directly with the social analysis. Modern society is its subject, but its approach is more exploratory than prescriptive. The closed story defines its own moral, but within the context of a larger complexity. Gorald's death is only an episode in Birkins life. The open story is the more inclusive of the two, and to recognize this is to see the vital role in the novel of speculation, choice, quest and incompletion.

In Lawrence's little read, brilliantly extended introduction to Maurice Magnus' Memories of the Foreign Legion, we encounter this passage:

> "Why!" I said "Is it you?"
>
> "Yes," he replied. "A terrible things has happened".
>
> He waited on the stairs, and I went down. Rather unwillingly, because I detest terrible things, and the people to whom they happen.
>
> The people to whom they happen. Put this phrase beside an early exchange between Birkin and Gerald in Women in Love:
>
> "You think people should just do as they like".
>
> "I think they always do".[42]

Put these two together, and we are at the very centre of the starting development that the old idea that "Character is fate" achieves in Lawrence, and particularly here in Women in Love. If we consider this development in relation to the uses of the same idea in earlier novels. We will see just how it is startling. Over a third of the Portrait of a lady, for example, is "taken up with brushwork", according to Stephen Spenders mistaken reading, "That has nothing to do with the story". Really, James is painting in all the features of Isabel Archer's lovely, can did intelligence which is yet an intelligence where every virtue shades off into not perhaps, a vice, but at least a false perception-all this so that we can recognize the inevitability of her renunciation of the right to ignorance once her education is corruption is completed, and she gains her moral freedom in the paradox of social slavery. This is among our finest demonstrations in fiction of the belief in the freedom of the will and the responsibilities of that freedom – a belief necessarily selects for its emphasis the concept character from the whole phrase character is fate. In Lawrence, the two terms become equivalents, the emphasis distributed with complete equality and balance. The new development in Lawrence is found most clearly in his theme of the victim who invites the victimizer, the murderer who invites the murderer, because the equivalence of these terms had not previously been handled in fiction, and because of the extremity with which Lawrence felt the urgency of this interpretation for the modern world. The idea that we can and constantly do choose our fate, not only our social or our psychological fate, but our final fate, our destiny, choose life or death- because of the novelty of this interpretation in fiction and the extremity with which Lawrence felt it, he abandoned the kind of novel he had been writing and the kinds of novel that had been written by others, and attempted instead to write the novel as psychic drama. He first become aware of the alteration in his aims as he was writing The Rainbow; he become completely aware of it as he was writing Women in Love. The change can be seen in four ways:

> First in characterization. The whole notion of character in fiction undergoes an alteration. He will now create more essential eings, will be concerned first of all not with the "ego" that interests the traditional novelist, but with the primal forces that are prior to character.
>
> ....I don't think the psychology is wrong, it is only that I have a different attitude to my characters and that necessitates a different attitude in you, which you are not prepared to give....... I don't care about physiology of matter – but somehow – that which is physic – no – human in humanity, is more interesting to me than the old fashioned human element – which causes one to conceive a character in a certain moral scheme and make him consistent. The certain moral scheme is what I object to. In Turgeneu, and in Tolstoy, and in Dostoevsky, the moral scheme into which all the characters fit – and it is nearly the

> same scheme whatever the extraordinariness of the characters themselves, dull, old, dead, when Marinetti writes:"..... The heat of a piece of wood or iron is in fact more passionate, for us, than the laughter or tears of a woman" – then I know what he means. He is stupid, as an artist, contrasting the heat of the iron and the laugh of the women..... I don't so much care about what the women feels – in the ordinary usage of the word. That presumes an ego to feel with. I only care about what the woman is – what she is – in humanly, physiologically, materially, according to the human conception. You mustn't look in my novels for the old stable ego of the character. There is another ego, according to whose action the individual is unrecognizable, and passes through, as it were, allotropic states which it needs a deeper sense than any other we have been used to exercise, to discover are states of the same single radically unchanged element.[43]

In the novel itself, Birkin tells us that personalities are not very interesting, that there are only a few great ideas that animate all individuals, these are the basic elements, the carbon, life and death, the two possible allegiances. And these are the psychic engagements that the novelist wishes to explore, just as they are the elements beneath the social character that interest Birkin informing his personal relationships:

> He looked at her, to see, if he felt that she was good looking.
>
> "I don't feel that you're good-looking", he said.
>
> "Not even attractive?" she mocked, bitingly.
>
> He knitted his brows in sudden exasperation.
>
> "Don't you see that it's not a question of visual appreciation in the least", he cried.

"I don't want to see you. I've seen plenty of women; I'm sick and weary of seeing them. I want a woman I don't see". "I'm sorry, I can't oblige you by being invisible", she laughed.

"Yes", he said, you are invisible to me, if you do not force me to be visually aware of you. But I don't want to see you or hear you.

What did you ask me to tea for, then? She mocked.

I want to find you, where you don't know your own existence, the you that your common self denies utterly. But don't want your good looks, and I don't want your womanly feelings and I don't want your thoughts, nor opinions nor your ideas they are all bagatelles to me". "Your are very conceited, Monsieur," she mocked..... "I think you want to tell me you love me, and you go all this way round to do it". "All right", he said, looking up with sudden exasperation." Oh go away then, and leave me alone. I don't want any more of your meretricious persiflage".

"Is it really persiflage?" She mocked, her face really relaxing into laugher. [44]

This quotation is even more helpful than Lawrence's letter to an understanding of the change that has come over his intention since Sons and Lovers, and certainly it points to his new problem as a novelist. I want to find you, where you don't know your own existence, that your common self-denies utterly. And all the rest all that attaches to the conscious, social character is it, for a novelist, "really persiflage," "meretricious persiflage"? If it is, then the novel as it was written before Lawrence had been built on persiflage, since its generic character depends on the development of conflict out of social materials, and if we took Lawrence's letter with complete literalness, or Birkin's ambition as a true equivalent to the ambition of Lawrence, the novelist, he would be directed toward such a novelistic disaster as Virginia Wolf's The Waves, albeit in his terms. So we may say at once that in the novel, the pure psychic drama is impossibility, and that we do not have that attempt here.

What we have, in fact, are several different orders of characterization, the orders that traditionally appear in the novel. We have a group of "free" characters, and a group of "bound" characters. The free characters are limited to four, who actively seek out their fate through the plot movement; the rest are all fixed in their social roles, and in rigid social scenes, and, except perhaps for Hermione and the elder Criches, are caricatures whose fate is sealed before the outset. These have all taken the way of death, and therefore they exist at the level of the social personality alone, and they are characterized by means of the familiar technique of caricature, maximum selection. But the free characters, the four, are compounded of a double drive, and it is here that the method of characterization is new and unfamiliar. They have their social existence and they have their psychic existence; the first is inevitably an expression of the second, but in the second lays their whole motivation. As two take the way of death, their social role becomes more and more important ("Civilized society is insane, reflects Constance Chatterley"). And as the two other take the way of life, their social role becomes less important, ceases, in fact, to exist. This has been Birkin's ambition and struggle throughout, the need to isolate him on the cliff of self-responsibility outside society yet not outside human relationship. "If I find I can live sufficiently by myself," he continued, "I shall give up my work altogether. It has become death to me. I don't believe in the humanity, I pretend to be part of, I don't care a straw for the social ideals I live by, I hate the dying organic form of social mankind – so it can't be anything but trumpery, to work at education. I shall drop it as soon as I am clear enough-tomorrow perhaps-and be by myself."[45]

> "What I want is a strange conjunction with you-" he said quietly; "—not meeting and mingling;-you are quite right; but an equilibrium, a pure balance of two single beings: as the stars balance each other."[46]

The attempt is by no means an entire success, as the final pages of the novel make quite clear, but because of the nature of the attempt, the characterization of Birkin is not an entire success, either. He, more exclusively than any of the others, embodies Lawrence's ambition to handle the carbon in character, his drama comes nearest to being the pure psychic drama, but for the very reason that his suffering and his struggle have no social objectification and cannot have, he tends to elude us as a novelistic being. The contrast with Gerald is instructive.

The second large difference between *Women in Love* and the traditional novel is in the notion of structure. The book is to have no "story" in the conventional sense; instead, it is developed in separate episodes, and these are only sporadically developed as "scenes." Yet these are meant to form a pattern of psychic relationships ("the form of some other rhythmic form"), a pattern of psychic movement with a large general rhythm, but without the objective or rationalized frame of the old novel.

Because it does not have this rationalized frame, Women in Love gives a first impression of much greater looseness and even aimlessness than it actually has, and if we can begin reading it, not as what it begins by seeming – a realistic novel- but if we can begin reading it, not as what it begins by seeming – a realistic novel – but as a drama of primal compulsions, a psychic symbolization, it will be seen to have its own kind of coherence, its own kind of organized – indeed, highly and complexly organized – structural presentation of them. It is a different kind of structure from Conrad's or James's or Hardy's, bearing, perhaps, a more immediate relationship to the art of dance than to the traditional art of fiction. As in dance, it develops through the shifting allegiances between the members, and the configuration of characters, their thematic signifying, is perhaps the strictest of all English novels.

The basic pattern is established at once: Gudrun feels drawn to Gerald; Ursula feels drawn to Birkin. Each of these males is presently seen in another relationship with females: Gerald with the Pussums, whom he destroys, as she wishes; Birkin with Hermione, who is determined to dominate him by force of her will. In the second chapter, Birkin enunciates the theme. There are no accidents, he says; death seeks death; individuation is life; between the two is a perilous balance. From this discussion emerges presently the double idea: of Will-victim and victimizer, and of Death, symbolized socially in the coal mines, intellectually in Bohemia, the two finally brought together in Loerke, the industrial artist; and of Being wholeness of function, symbolized first in the African statue, and throughout the novel by the natural order – flowers, animals.

Through this quartet of characters this theme will sound. We might glance at some of its variations. For it is of the basic essence of Lawrence's intuition; that these two poles are not fixed or static; they are fluid forces kind of psychical dialectic, and his relationships are not for a minute rigid. The pattern is fluid, as these two forces and their derivatives attract and repel.

Birkin and Hermione, for example, have had a long relationship. From its opiates to his being, Birkin is now feebly trying to detach himself; the conflict bursts into the open and Hermione beats him with a chunk of lapis. The next scene, the two girls at the railroad crossing and Gerald on his horse, demonstrates their allegiance, Gudrun's fascination, Ursula's horror at Gerald's cruel domination. Next, we find Birkin in a deathly mood still, and Ursula attracted by but resisting the "life" he offers, and it is in that resistance that she moves toward Hermione. The big scene of "The Water Party" clarifiers issues momentarily: it is an experience of literal death, and it pushes both Gerald and Birkin, in their differing responses, toward their own destinies; the two women respond accordingly. In Chapter XV, which follows, Ursula yearns toward real death as an escape from a living death in society, and, being at death's door, not life's she now hates Birkin. Birkin turns away, and in the next chapter, he invites Gerald to enter a pact of complete commitment, one to the other. Gerald declines this invitation, and in the next chapter, the great pivotal chapter, "The Industrial magnate," we are reminded why. This is at once an interlude and a keystone, a projection of individual failure into the fabric of the social structure. The old man (impotent love) is here opposed to Gerald (abstract hate) and between them is the defeated will of the mother. This is a superb image of industrial society in its psychic terms, all its self-defeating pulls exposed, in industry, harmony becomes organization, and Gerald, as "God of the machine," "converted the industry into a new and terrible purity"-which is death itself. An immediate contrast with the mechanical image is found in the next chapter, "Rabbit"-the image of the vital, wholly single, wholly self-possessed animal life. To Gerald and Gudrun, the creature is "mad," yet in their observation of it, they feel their own bond in some recognized "obscenity," Again, in this chain-like structure a contrast follows. The chapter called "Moony" shows us Ursula's conflict of despair and desire, to yield or to will; and Birkin's conflict between desire and destructiveness, in the elaborate moon image reflected on the water, which he attempts to destroy. But like life, it persists in reasserting itself. The conclusion is Birkin's decision to propose marriage to Urusla, but the proposal is a fiasco, and once more he withdraws. Meantime, how-ever, because the larger form of the "process" is working in both Ursual and Gudrun, through and above these variation, they draw apart, begin to feel their alienation. As they draw apart, Birkin once more turns to Gerald, having been denied by Ursula, and if we feel anything legitimated to the novel's purpose in the chapter called "Gladiatorial," we feel Lawrence's own sense of the desperateness of his psychic dialectic in this symbolic conflict. "Woman to Woman" is a counterpart to the chapter called "Man to Man" and shows us Urusla and Hermione in momentary allegiance against Birkin. The Urusal-birking climax comes in the chapter called "Excurse," in Birkin's self-recognition, and in the achievement of their "polarity" in relationship.

The other side of the story now develops contrariwise. In "death and love," the death of Gerald's father drives him to Gudrun, by way of the graveyard; he brings the clay of his father's new grave into her bedroom. This is love as death, and the process now need only resolve itself, as it quickly does. The four go abroad. Ursula and Birkin find the cold Alps uncongenial and leave; Gudrun pits her will against Gerald. She is on the way to becoming a Hermione, but because here is the death seeking, not the life-seeking antagonist, Gudrun wins: she kills him, which is also what he has sought. And the novel ends on the partial resolution found by Ursula and Birkin. It seems to say that they have found as much as can be expected by any two individuals unless more individuals will make their effort.

It is instructive to compare this fluid, dance-like movement with the characteristic structure of Thomas Hardy, as, for example, in Jude the Obscure. The scheme here is a kind of rigidly counter pointed interchange of character that Hardy much enjoyed. He begins with Jude and Arabella. Then he sets up Sue and Philotson. Then Jude and Sue reverse their original partners. It is like a folkdance figure, and Hardy's interest is in making it come full circle; it is perfectly expressive of the iron morality that obsessed his imagination.

> The certain moral scheme is what I object to, Lawrence declared, and referred, of course, not to Hardy, but to that social morality with which most novelists, including Hardy, have generally been concerned, and of which the traditional notion of plot is an expression. Lawrence wishes to explore a deeper life, a life that seethes and boils beneath institutions as it seethes and boils beneath "personalities."[47]

This is the third great difference between 'Women in Love' and other novels. The structure of the novel is so precisely and so richly expressive of this theme that, after even a cursory examination of the structure, little more need be said of theme, but we should observe how explicit Lawrence is in enunciating it. Halfway through the novel we come upon this exact antithesis:

> Birking thought of Gerald. He was one of those strange white wonderful demons from the north, fulfilled in the destructive frost mystery. And was he fated to pass in this knowledge, this one process of frost-knowledge, death by perfect cold? Was he a messenger, an omen of the universal dis-solution into whiteness and snow?

> Birkin was frightened. He was tired, too, when he had reached this length of speculation. Suddenly his strange, strained attention gave way, he could not attend to these mysteries any more. There was another way, the way of freedom. There was the paradisal entry into pure, single being, the individual soul taking precedence over love and desire for union, stronger than any pangs of emotion, a lovely state of free proud singleness, which accepted the obligation of the permanent connection with others, and with the other, submits to the yoke and leash of love, but never forfeits its own proud individual singleness, even while it loves and yields.

The relationships of the novel are founded on this opposition, on the idea of death and life and death in life; and the characters move entirely in terms of these two impulses, their conflicts and their embraces developing out of their allegiance to one or the other. Love is, of course, Lawrence's focus, since he wished to say that in modern life we use love for death-purposes more frequently than we do for life-purposes. ("The point about love is that we hate the word because we have vulgarized it. It ought to be prescribed, tabooed from utterance, for many years, till we get a new, better idea.") Lawrence's theme, as we have suggested, is dramatized in terms of a struggle between what he calls 'Will' (which may be either sensual or "spiritual." A death impulse in either case) and 'Being', that integration of the total self which is life. 'Will' is the integration of the drive of ego toward power, toward domination; it has its inverse in the desire to be overpowered, to be dominated, to yield everything to dissolution. 'Will' is mechanical, and its symbol is therefore the machine; its historical and social embodiment is an industrial society that lives by war. 'Being' is the integration of life forces in total and complete self-responsibility. Its historical embodiment lives in the future.

Lawrence had, of course a conviction that the novel can still do what it has never done in the past. It is a conviction that follows upon his generally prophetic purpose. In the ninth chapter of Lady Chatterley's Lover, he says that the novel "can inform and lead into new places the How of our sympathetic consciousness, and it can lead our sympathy away in recoil from things gone dead." The two elements here point to the two major technical developments in this novel; the concern with the future, with the smashing of dead patterns and the release of life into new ones, has direct effect in the concept of structure and the use of structure that we have examined; the attempt to make a direct approach to our "sympathetic consciousness" has an immediate effect in Lawrence's sense of language and his use of language. The fourth difference, then is in the style of Women in Love, and particularly in the visionary quality that is generated by the style.

An appeal to our "sympathetic consciousness" must be absolutely direct as direct as music or dance. We must be made to feel this conflict not in our intellects but in our nerves, as it were, if it is to mean anything at all. Lawrence argues throughout, of course, but the only effective argument is in the direct presentation, which comes to us, if it does, trough the style. This, Lawrence seemed to know, since he deliberately attempts, first of all, a kind of incantatory prose through the use of repetition, a kind of drugged choral quality, which is perhaps what E.M. Forster had in mind when he said that Lawrence was the only modern novelist "in whom song predominates, who has the rapt bardic quality." It is Forster, too, who speaks of the achievement of Lawrence's style as the "irradiation of the universe and the objects that compose it." This would have to do with diction and figure rather than with rhythm, and we can perhaps see the intention in the high use of color, and in the resulting spectacular quality of the images and of the flitting scene:

> ".....through the man in the closed wagon Gudrun could see the whole scene spectacularly, isolated and momentary, like a vision isolated in eternity."[48]

There are a description of the best moments in the novel-scenes such as that where the whole party goes bathing:

> ....The first to run across the lawn was the little Italian, small and like a cat, her white legs twinkling as She went, ducking slightly her head, that was tied in a gold silk kerchief, she tripped through the gate and down the grass, and stood, like a tiny figure of ivory and bronze, at the water's edge, having dropped off her twirling, watching the swans, which came up in surprise. Then out ran Miss Bradley, like a large, soft plum in her dark-blue suit. Then Gerald came, a scarlet sill kerchief round his Joins, his towel over his arms. He seemed to flaunt himself a little in the sun, lingering and laughing, strolling easily, looking white but natural in his nakedness. Then Sir Joshua, in an overcoat, and lastly Hermione, striking with stiff grace from out of a great mantle of purple silk, her head tied up in purple and gold. Handsome was her stiff, long body, her straight-stepping white legs, there was a static magnificence about her as she let the cloak float loosely away from her striding. She crossed the lawn like some strange memory, and passed slowly towards the water.[51]

Attempts at this quality of the spectacular, of the hallucinated, are not always successful; certainly the three women dancing in Oriental costumes conveniently provided do not quite get into the convention that Lawrence is trying to develop, and the scene of Gudrun, doing her

Dalcroze rhythms in the presence of the livestock, does not quite escape the ridiculous. Yet we must recognize, all through the novel, this attempt at the spectacular, the eternally isolated, which leads to the hallucinated effects, and throughout to the strangely irritating compulsive qualities of dreams:

> ....She put her hand on the arm of her care-worn, sallow father and frothing her light draperies, preceded over the eternal red carpet. Her father, mute and yellowish, his black beard making him look more care-worn, mounted the steps stiffly, as if his spirit were absent; but the laughing mist of the bride went along with him undiminished.
>
> And no bridegroom had arrived! It was intolerable for her, Ursula, her heart strained with anxiety, was watching the hill beyond; the white, descending road that should give sight of him. There was a carriage. It was running. It had just come into sight. Yes, it was he. Ursula turned towards the bride and the people, and, from her place of vantage, gave an inarticulate cry. She wanted to warn them that he was coming. But her cry was inarticulate and inaudible, and she flushed deeply, between her desire and her wincing confusion.[50]

To this development of style we should add the insistent contrast of the diction between the mechanical and the organic, and the attempt of the style to persuade us of the force inhering in all life, says in his own preface. "In point of style, fault is often found with the continual, slightly modified repetition. The only answer is that it is natural to the author; and that every natural crisis in emotion or passion or understanding comes from this pulsing, frictional to and which works up to culmination." The attempt to duplicate, in syntactical movement itself, the dialectical flow of the themes is perhaps a mistaken aesthetic ambition, but we should observe it as part of Lawrence's particular kind of integrity as an artist.

The intention of Women in Love is so tremendous, so central to our lives, that we must for our own sakes make an effort to tolerate it. I say tolerate for the reason that I have known almost no readers who, on first reading, did not find it either opaque beyond endurance, or tiresome, or revolting. This has been the response even of readers who can agree with Lawrence when he in effect equates plot as we have known it with a morality that has lost its relevance, even its reality. Yet, is it not the fact that the reason the novel is difficult to judge is that it will not accept the disciplines of plot, but does not quite find some new limitation that will contain this material, so that we are repeatedly asked to love Lawrence the man in order to accept Lawrence the novelist? Scenes like that in which Birkin invites Gerald to be his blood brother, repulsive to our social sense, grotesque before our literary taste, simply say. "Take me at my own level of sincerity, of seriousness, and not at yours, and you will see that this is exactly right." And the question is whether a novelist has the right to impose himself to this extent on his reader, even when his reader is eager to accept as much as he can, even when his reader, like the present writer, cannot, after eight or ten readings of this novel, imagine being without it. It is possible that Women in Love attempts to do more than the novel as we know it and even as Lawrence developed it knows how to do. This does not for a moment mean that the attempt must not be made. No novelist speaks more directly to us than Lawrence, and if we can't hear him, we are, I quite believe, lost. But he has not, in this book, found the whole way to speak. His attempt to move into the realm of psychic drama we can take seriously in a way that we cannot take the diluted attempt of

Virgina Wolf; but can we always hear what Lawrence wants us to hear? The question is not whether he is right; the question is: What is a novel?

> Judging Women in Love in its own terms as a single work, I should say that its success is partial; judging it as a step in a career, I should remove the qualification. It is perhaps the most important single work in Lawrence's formal education.[51]

If we follow him on from Women in Love, through the next really shattered books, and to the end, we will see that he took, finally, two ways: in his last two books, 'Lady Chatterley's Lover' and The Man Who Died both, in my view, very great books he divided the intention that in Women in Love is one. In Lady Chatterley, he retrenches his claims a little-it is a novel in a solid and sustained social context, and it is a novel with a clear and happily developed plot, in which characters function fully and the author lets them speak for themselves; In The Man Who Died, he make an absolutely unqualified claim for the sanctify of the purely self-responsible individual human being, society not more than a shadowy threat outside the novel, and he gives us a real image of what he does not give us in Birkin, the wholly integrated man; but he writes in the form of the fable.

For the novel always drags us back into the world, into circumstance Conrad says that "the energy of evil is so much more forcible than the energy of good," and perhaps this is because in novels, at least, pure evil does not exist whereas there are those novelists who attempt to make pure good prevail. Those who read-those who can stay to read Women in Love to the last fifty pages-the death of Gerald in the snow and the grievous pathos of Birkin without him-those readers come, I think, upon fifty pages that have more power of a particular kind than any other fifty pages in any other English or American novel. It is what we might call the real Russian bang. But Gerald is not the saint, he is the sinner, he is-us; and as we can see in reading novels in some ways so different as 'Middlemarch' and The Wings of the Dove, sinners for the very reason that the novel as we have so far known it is a genre that deals with individuals in a social context sinners it can save for art, but its saints are damned.

V. LADY CHATTERLEY'S LOVER

As a novelist, Lawrence felt he should be concerned not so much with depicting social change as with making conscious the changing thoughts and feelings within the individual. But this change in emphasis should not be taken to imply that he has gone back on his previous novel. He still believes in fighting for "whole consciousness", which was Roman's aim; and if the stress in Lady Chatterley's Lover is on "phallic consciousness", which is "vital part" of whole consciousness in man, this is because he found that the "irritable cerebral consciousness" had been exalted at the expenses of "the real phallic consciousness and spontaneity".[52] The fight, therefore, has to be waged on behalf of "the phallic reality", though the aim is to attain a balance between the mind and the body, and to bring them into a harmonious relationship. Lady Chatterley's Lover was conceived by Lawrence as "a novel contrasting the mental consciousness with the phallic consciousness"[53], and it is the conflict between these two modes of consciousness which gives the novel its formal structure:

> As I say, it is a novel of the phallic Consciousness: or the phallic Consciousness versus the mental– spiritual Consciousness: and of course you know which side I take. The versus is not my fault; there should be no versus. The two things must be reconciled in us. [54]

Lawrence considered the phallus to be a great sacred image representing "a deep, deep life which has been denied in us"[55]; and it was his sincere belief he wrote to Harriet Monroe – that the phallic consciousness must be restored into our lives, because.

> It is the source of all real beauty, and all real gentleness. And those are the two things, tenderness and beauty, which will save us from horrors.... And in my novel I work for them directly, and direct from the phallic consciousness, which, you understand, am not the cerebral sex-consciousness, but something really deeper, and root of poetry, lived or sung.[56]

The distinction made here between the phallic consciousness and the cerebral sex-consciousness should in no case be lost sight of, for it is the "warm, blood-sex", which establishes the living and vitalizing connection between man and woman, that Lawrence believed in – not the modern sex which "is a pure matter of nerves, cold and bloodless". Whereas the phallic reality is warm and spontaneous, "sex is a thing that exists in the head, its reactions are cerebral, and its processes mental". This sex which is "a mental reaction nowadays and hopelessly cerebral affair", Lawrence found ugly and repulsive. "And I, who loathe sexuality so deeply", he said in a letter in exasperation, "am considered a lurid sexuality specialist."[57] In Lady Chatterley's Lover, his "nice and tender phallic novel" Lawrence attempted to show how the sex relation can be "valid and precious" instead of being shameful. To the woman whom Lawrence had given the manuscript of his novel to type, and who had refused to go on typing after the first few pages because she found it too indecent, he wrote: "And remember, although you are on the side of the angels and the vast majority, mine is the truly moral and religious position."[58] Such was the misunderstanding of his intention-conscious intention, at any rate – in writing the book, that he had to reiterate time and again that he had not pandered to the pornographic taste, that he was not advocating "perpetual sex", that he was not suggesting that women should "go running after gamekeepers" or after anybody, that he more than anybody else deplored cheap, promiscuous, heartless sex. "Nothing nauseates me more than promiscuous sex in and out of season", he wrote to Ottoline Morrell. His purpose in writing Lady Chatterley's Lover, he continued, was "to make an adjustment in consciousness to the basic physical realities". For the modern man and woman, he believed, the full, conscious realization of sex (i.e. "warm blood desire") was of the utmost importance. "And this is the real point of this book", he wrote in "A Propos of Lady Chatterley's Lover, "I want men and women to be able to think sex, fully, completely, honestly, and cleanly." (Sex, that is, which is a delicate flow of blood sympathy – not the "nervous, personal, disintegrative sort." Care must be taken to distinguish between the two different sense in which Lawrence uses the word "sex" – the way he himself understands it, and the way he thinks the "Moderns" do. As he puts it himself: "It is a mistake I have made, talking of sex I have always inferred that sex meant blood-sympathy and blood – contact. Technically this is so. But as a matter of fact, nearly all modern sex is a pure matter of nerves, cold and bloodless."[59] There should be a balance and harmony between the consciousness of body's sensations and experiences and these body's sensations and experiences themselves:

> And if I write a book about the sex relation of a man and women, it is not because I want all men and woman to begin having indiscriminate love affairs, off the reel....
>
> What you have to do is to get out of the state of funk,

> sex funk. And to do so, you've got to be perfectly decent, and you have to accept sex fully in the consciousness. Accept sex in the consciousness, and the normal physical awareness comes back, between you and other people..... t is the most important thing just now, this gentle physical awareness. It keeps us tender and alive at a moment when the great danger is to go brittle, hard, and in some way dead.[60]

Some of the subsidiary, though not unimportant, points in Lady Chatterley's Lover, (such as: what happened on the "night of sensual passion"? How successful or justified is Lawrence's use of "four-letter words"?) have been the subject of so much controversy and critical attention in recent years that it needs to be emphasized that the theme of the novel is tenderness in human relationships (Lawrence at one time wanted to change the title of his novel to Tenderness). The sexual scenes between Connie and Mellors in the later part of the novel have the kind of significance they have in the story only in the context of what we are told in the earlier part of the book.

The novel begins with the words:

"Ours is essentially a tragic age..." In what sense is our age essentially tragic? The tragic conception of life, in Lawrence's view, arose when "the grand idealists" Buddha, Plato, and Jesus-destroyed for man his "great relationships with the circumambient universe by their teaching that "the only happiness lay in abstracting oneself from life". Men and women today are almost totally abstracted from the world they live in and are reduced to mere separate personalities. We no longer know the world in togetherness with ourselves our knowledge is almost exclusively mental, rational, scientific knowledge in apartness. The great saviors and teachers only cut us off from "the rhythmic life

> of the seasons, birth and death and fruition", and turned us into "separate little entities". When we first meet the three principal characters in the novel Connie, Clifford, and Mellors – each of them is a separate, isolated individual, having no living relationship with anything or anybody. Clifford remains to the end isolated and apart, enclosed within his life of cerebral consciousness and its dead relationships; whereas for the other two there is the possibility that they might find some "religious and poetic" meaning in their life of togetherness, with its changing, developing relationships.[61]

In Lady Chatterley's Lover, Lawrence has dramatized the conflict between two modes of consciousness – cerebral and phallic; and between two kinds of relationships – dead and living.

Sir Clifford is presented in the novel as a character who has lost all connection with his fellow men and women. He is alone and isolated, incapable of any "togetherness". He has overdeveloped his mental consciousness at the expense of his "emotional and human life". In all this he can be said to be "a pure product of our civilization. To some extent we are all part of his civilization, and to that extent we are all Clifford's and hence targets of the novel's attack. In criticizing Clifford and what he stands for Lawrence contrary to the popular belief was criticizing not just an individual or a social class, nor even a "type", but an attitude, and an aspect of the civilization of which he himself was so much a part. If he shows no "pity" for Clifford and is unsparing in his condemnation of him, this is because he is castigating a part of himself. Diana Trilling– though the expression "extreme cruelty" used by her seems to me a bit too strong – is undoubtedly right when she says:

> Everybody knows Lawrence was representing an image of himself in the gamekeeper Mellors in Lady Chatterley's Lover. But Lawrence was not only Mellors in that novel, he was Clifford Chatterley as well. This is what licenses his quite extreme cruelty to Clifford Chatterley.[62]

This has the support of Frieda Lawrence also who has remarked that "the terrible thing about Lady C. is that Lawrence identified himself with both Clifford and Mellors".[63] Lawrence is not "kind" to Clifford, whose own "Kindness" is, underneath, mere coldness of heart: but his attitude is not without real, discriminating sympathy. For even satire is a form of sympathy. It was Lawrence's passionate concern for the future of mankind which made him show up Clifford for what he is – for Clifford, after all, only forms a part of the "New race of mankind," over-conscious in the money and social and political side, on the spontaneous, intuitive side dead, but dead. Half-corpses, all of them but with a terrible insistent consciousness in the other half.

Clifford marries Connie during the war when he is home for a month on leave. Then he goes back to Flanders, only to be shipped back home again six months later "More or less in bits". He gradually recovers and is able to return to life again, but "with the lower half of his body, from the hips down, paralyzed for ever". Why did Lawrence make Clifford paralyzed? In "A Propos of Lady Chatterley's Lover" he says:

> The lameness of Clifford was symbolic of the paralysis, of most men of his sort and class today. I realized that it was perhaps taking an unfair advantage of Connie, to paralyze him technically. It made it so much more vulgar of her to leave him.[64]

The paralysis of Clifford, as Lawrence explains in a letter also, is symbolic in the sense in which "all art is symbolic, conscious or unconscious." He had not deliberately worked symbolically, but the character of Clifford as it took shape in his imagination turned out to be an apt symbol of the over intellectualized and emotionally paralyzed humanity of the day, and Lawrence recognized the unconscious symbolism later on.

The criticism the novel makes of Clifford is also the substance of Lawrence's attack on modern civilization with its preponderance of "cerebral consciousness". Most modern men and women, as Lawrence saw with dismay, had been turned into half-corpses: they were most of them, notwithstanding all the "machine fucking" (as Mellors puts it) that goes on, paralysed in "the emotional and humanly-individual part". It was Lawrence's concern for his fellow men and women who had – so he believed – gone nearly dead in so far as their affective life was concerned, which made Lawrence intensify his attack on over-intellectualization in modern life.

When Clifford and Connie are married, the sex part does not mean much to either of them-though apart from this they are very close together in an intimacy which is deep and "beyond sex". Sex seems to them merely an accident, an adjunct – "one of the curious obsolete, organic processes which persisted in its own clumsiness, but was not really necessary. Then with the injury received in the war Clifford is so much hurt that "something inside him was perished, some of his feelings had gone. There was a blank of insentience."[65] Whatever warmth of heart was there in him is killed by the war. When he comes to live in Wragby hall, he has very little connection with other people; he is not really in touch with anyone. Connie feels even she cannot really touch him, since in the last issue he is "just a negation of human contact. In this state he takes to writing stories – stories that are cleverly written but are "in some mysterious way, meaningless". Even in the stories there is "no touch, no actual contact." These smart stories are something new and "entirely personal" and have "no organic connection with the thought and expression that had gone before. But his writing brings him fame and success; and success – the bitch-goddess. Success, as Tommy Dukes calls it, after Henry James – restores to him his confidence and his equanimity. He is surrounded at Wragby Hall by his old Cambridge friends, young intellectuals who all "believed in the life of mind". Connie has to listen to these "highly mental gentlemen" making their "immensely important" speculations and using "millions of words, in the parade of the life of mind". She finds it fun, to a certain extent. "But what cold minds"; Even Tommy Dukes, who expresses some of Lawrence's own views, is a mere windbag. "Talk, talk, talk. What hell it was the continual rattle of it". All that can be said in Dukes's favor is that he is at least honest in his thinking. As far as words go, his utterances are not unlike those of his creator. "Real knowledge" he says, "comes out of the whole corpus of the consciousness; out of your belly and your penis as much as out of your brain and mind. The mind can only analyse and rationalize." But as he says himself he is "only a 'mental-lifer. His intellectual beliefs are all right, but when it comes to deeds, he feels he cannot really want a woman: "I just simply can't vibrate in unison with a woman." Julian Moynahan finds the presence of Clifford's cronies in the novel superfluous. Even Dukes, he says, only anticipate the views of Mellors who needs no "press gentry" as he can very well "speak for himself".[66] It is odd that Moynahan should have failed to see what has been made so obvious in accordance with their words. As Lawrence puts it in "A Propos". it is The

Deed of life we have now to learn: we are supposed to have learnt the Word, but alas, look at us, "Word-perfect we may be, but Deed – demented." The title of Moynahan's book, The Deed of Life, is, ironically, taken from this quotation:

> As years go by Connie feels the bruise of fear and horror coming up and spreading in Clifford. "The bruise was deep, deep.......... The bruise of the false inhuman war." Clifford is still quite alert, mentally: but the paralysis, the bruise of the great shock was gradually spreading in the affective self. Seeing the "background of his mind" fill up with nothingness, Connie dimly realizes "one of the great laws of the human soul."
>
> That when the emotional soul receives a wounding shock, which does not kill the body, the soul seems to recover as the body recovers. But this is only appearance. It is really on the mechanism of the re-assumed habit. Slowly the wound to the soul begins to make itself felt, like a bruise, which only slowly deepens its terrible ache, till it fills all the psyche. And when we think we have recovered and forgotten, it is then that the terrible after-effects have to be encountered at their worst.[67]

Clifford tends to fall into fits of depression and to go vague and absent. Connie realizes that it is "the wound to his psyche coming out." But there is nothing she can do about it. It is only later when Clifford begins to take an interest in the mines that he feels a new sense of power coming into him:

> It gave him a sense of power, of power. He was doing something: and he was going to do something. He was going to win, to win, not as he had won with

> his stories, mere publicity amid a whole sapping of energy and malice. But a man's victory.[68]

Clifford's success in the field of industrial activity is undoubted. As a practical man and a master, he proves to be amazingly astute and powerful. This, in itself, goes to his credit: but, and this is the substance of Lawrence's criticism, this success is attained at the expense of his emotional and human life. While he is mastering the technicalities of modern coal-mining, he lets his humanly-individual part go pulpy, and becomes "almost a creature, with a hard, efficient shell of an exterior and a pulpy interior, one of the amazing crabs and lobsters of modern industrial and financial world, invertebrates of the crustacean order, with shells of steel, like machines, and inner bodies of soft pulp. No wonder, then, that he comes to believe that" "the industry comes before the individual."[69]

Connie, when she marries Clifford, has had her tentative love affairs based on "all the passion of mental attraction" and has learnt to take the "sex-thrill" as a sensation without in the least yielding her "pure and noble freedom," which, to her, is "infinitely more wonderful than any sexual love Her relationship with Clifford develops into a deep personal intimacy because "unlike other young men "who insisted on the sex thing like dogs", he is not just keen on his "satisfaction".[70] When he returns home crippled, she sticks to him passionately because he has been hurt so much. Their intimacy, however, is an affair of the mind only; they cannot even bring themselves to talk to each other on matters concerning their bodily existence. "They were so intimate, and utterly out of touch." Connie has no contact with other people at Wragby, either; has no "real connection" with them. Her existence seems to her "all a dream", or a simulacrum of reality.

> Time went on. Whatever happened, nothing happened, because she was so beautifully out of contact. She and Clifford lived in their ideas and his books....... Time went on as the clock does, half-past eight instead of half-past seven.[71]

To escape the restlessness arising out of her "disconnection" she starts going to the wood: but even the wood is no real refuge or sanctuary for her as she has no connection with it. She never really touches the "spirit of the wood." She becomes vaguely aware that she has lost all touch with "the substantial and vital world". Knowing what torture Clifford would feel at the slightest sign of flirtation on her part, she gives no encouragement to the men who are nice and attentive to her, and remains "quiet and vague". Then comes Michaelis, "the outsider," himself a lonely figure, out of contact with his surroundings and she gives herself to him out of sheer compassion and sympathy for him. "To her it meant nothing except" that she gave herself to him. He also rouses in her "a wild, craving physical desire,"[72] which, however, he cannot satisfy, "he was always come and finished so quickly, then shrinking down on her breast, and recovering somewhat his effrontery while she lay dazed, disappointed, lost. But she knows how to get her sexual thrill out of him; she has not forgotten what she had learnt as young girl at Dresden—that she only had to hold herself back in sexual intercourse, and let him finish and expend himself without herself coming to the crisis: and then she could prolong the connection and achieve her orgasm and her crisis while he was merely her tool.

When Michaelis points out to her that Clifford is "entirely wrapped up in himself" and has really no use for her, she can see the truth in this. Her marriage with Clifford is now little more than "the long slow habit of intimacy, formed through years of suffering and patience." Clifford's ideas about marriage, even his desire for a son, seem to her curiously impersonal: all his talk about "integrated life" and about arranging "this sex thing as we arrange going to the dentist seems to her mere words, meaning really nothing.

> The only reality was nothingness, and over it a hypocrisy of words. She feels an inward dread and emptiness gradually spreading in her. Yet when Michaelis suggests her leaving Clifford, she cannot agree. "it may seem to you Clifford doesn't count", she tells him, but he does. When you think how disabled he is and sensual satisfaction is not enough to lure her away form her life with Clifford; and if later on she decides to abandon him, it is in exchange for a whole new life of emotions, warmth, and tenderness that her relationship with Mellor's brings to her. The short-lived affair with Michaelis comes to an end........ sneering voice," You couldn't go off at the same time as a man, when on one occasion, after they have made love, he tells her in a bitter mind could you? You'd have to bring yourself off! You'd have to run the show!" Connie is stunned by this unexpected piece of brutality.[73]

This speech was one of the crucial blows of Connie's life. It killed something in her. She had not been so very keen on Michaels, till he started it, she did not want him. It was as if she never positively wanted him. But once he had started her, it seemed only natural for her to come to her own crisis with him...... Her whole sexual feeling for him, or for a man, collapsed that night, her life fell apart from his as completely as if he had never existed.

> And she went through the days drearily. There was nothing now but this empty treadmill of what Clifford called the integrated life; the long living together of

> two people, who are in the habit of being in the same house with one "another, nothingness."
>
> Into this life of "nothingness" comes the gamekeeper "like a sudden rush of a threat out of nowhere. Like other characters in the novel he is, as Connie observes, a "separate fellow", aloof, apart, a man very much alone and on his own, "a creature purely alone." Yet there is also certain warmth about him, and it is this which starts in Connie a weary yearning and a sense of dissatisfaction with her life. As she looks one day at her reflexion in the mirror, the sight of her naked body turning "grayish and shapless" arouses in her a deep sense of injustice and a cold indignation against Clifford and "all the men of his sort who defrauded a woman even and body." In a way, she knows poor Clifford is not to blame. "His was the greater misfortune." It is, she recognizes, all part of a general catastrophe.[76]

And yet was he not in a way to blame? This lack of warmth, this lack of the simple, warm, physical contact, was he not to blame for that? He was never really warm, not even kind, only thoughtful considerate in a well-bred, cold sort of way! But never warm as a man can be warm to a woman.

> In devoting her life to Clifford Connie begins to wonder, is she not sacrificing herself to" a cold spirit of vanity that had no warm human contacts"? But even now when Michaelis proposes that she should marry him and get divorced from Clifford, she cannot do it: her "heart simply stood still at the thought of abandoning Clifford there and then. She couldn't do it. No...no!
>
> She just couldn't
>
> However, finding that she is "so utterly out of touch" with Clifford ("He never took her hand and held it

free creative self-expression at all levels by every living human being. He warns us against the trend towards destruction implicit in a machine driven civilization, leading on to both moral and physical death. Indeed, Lawrence was not only concerned with modern, industrial civilization of the west but with its entire Platonic – Christian heritage– a fact which is often not appreciated, and offers a non-repressive alternative, to the western cul-de-sac. The alternative vision is rooted in the un-self conscious acceptance of critical and aggressive instincts and a living awareness of the non-human universe.

Thus Lawrence essentially remains a socio-moral novelist and the methodology he employs to achieve his aim is psychoanalysis. No novelist or poet has been more concerned with the representation of human reality than D.H. Lawrence. To this end at times he appears to have by passed art and interpose nothing between the reader and his vision. All the readers of Lawrence may not agree with his philosophy, with his remedies of social ills he so effectively diagnosed, but they will certainly find some important areas of agreement. For any one interested in thinking about how to live life wholly and seriously, his novels are a remarkable testament.

BIBLIOGRAPHY

I. Works by D.H. Lawrence

(A) Letters and Essays

Assorted Articles, London (Martin Secker), 1930.

The Collected Letters of D.H. Lawrence, ed., Harry T. Moore (2 vols.) London (Heinemann), 1962.

Fantasia of the Unconscious and Psychoanalysis and the Unconscious, Phoenix Edition. London (Heinemann), 1961.

The Letters of D.H. Lawrence, ed. Aldus Huxley. London (Heinemann) 1956.

Phoenix: *The Posthumous Papers of D.H. Lawrence*, ed. Edward D. McDonald. London (Heinemann) 1961.

"Prologue to Women in Love (Unpublished)", in Texas Quarterly, VI (1963), I, pp. 98-III.

Selected Literary Criticism, ed., Anthony Beal. London (Heinemann) 1956.

Sex, Literature and Censorship, ed., Harry T. Moore. London (Heinemann) 1955.

Studies in Classic American Literature, Phoenix Edition London (Heinemann), 1955.

(B) Novels and Short Stories

Unless otherwise noted, all works listed are in the Phoenix Edition (Heineman).

Aaron's Rod, London 1954.

Apocalypse, Florene (U.Orioli) 1931 – London (Martin Secker) 1932.

The Complete Short Stories (3 Vols), London 1956.

Kangaroo, London 1955.

Lady Chatterley's Lover, London 1963.

The Lost Girl, London 1955.

Mornings in Mexico and Etruscan Places, London 1956.

The Plumed Serpent, London 1955.

The Rainbow, London 1955.

The Short Novels, (2 vols). London 1956.

D.H. Lawrence, Sons and Lovers, London, 1956,

The Trespasser, London 1955.

Twilight in Italy, Pocket Edition, London (Heinemann) 1954.

The White Peacock, London 1955.

Women in Love, New York (London Library) n.d. London 1960.

(C) Poems

The Complete Poems (3 Vols.), Phoenix Edition. London (Heinemann) 1957.

II. Biographical and Critical Studies

The Achievement of D.H. Lawrence, Eds. Frederick J. Hoffman And Harry T. Moore Norman (University of Oklahoma Press) 1953.

Abington, Richard. "A Wreath For Lawrence", In Encounter, Xvi, Iv (April 1960) Pp. 51-4.

Beal, *Anthony. D.H Lawrence*, Writers And Critics Series. Edinburgh (Oliver & Boyd) 1961.

Beebe, *Maurice*, "Lawrence's Sacred Fount: The Artist Theme of Sons and Lovers", in Texas Studies In Literature and Language, N, pp. 539-52.

Daiches, David, *The Novel and the Modern World,* Chicago (University Press) 1960.

Daleskl, H.M. *The Forked Flame: A Study of D.H. Lawrence,* London (Faber) 1965.

Draderf, R. P. "Authority and the Individual: A Study of D.H. Lawrence's 'Kangaroo", In The Critical Quarterly. I, Iii, pp. 208-15.

E.T. [Jessie (Chabers) Wood]. D.H. Lawrence: A Personal Record London (Cape), 1935.

Edel, Leon, "The Rainbow: Fiddle-Bow And Sand", In Essays in Criticism, Xi (1961) pp. 418-34.

Hough, Graham. The Dark Sun: A Study Of D.H. Lawrence. London (Gerald Duckworth), 1956.

Japheth-Kerr, Martin [Tiverton, Father. William] D.H. Lawrence and Human Existence. London (Scm Press) 1951.

Kettle, Arnold. An Introduction to The English Novel, Vol. Ii. London (Arrow Books), 1962.

D.H. Lawrence: A Collection of Critical Essays, Ed. Mark Spilka. Englewood (Liffs, J.J. (Prentice-Hall) 1963.

Lawrence, Frieda. The Memoirs and Correspondence, Ed. E.V. Tedlock. London (Heinemann), 1961.

Leavis, F.R. D.H. Lawrence Novelist. London (Chatto & Windus) 1955.

Moore, Harry, T. The Intelligent Heart. London (Heinemann) 1955.

—The Life And Works of D.H. Lawrence. London (Unwin Books) 1963.

Moynahan, Julian. The Deed of Life: The Novels And Tales of D.H. Lawrence London (Oxford University Press) 1963.

Murry, J. Middleton. Between Two Worlds. London (Cape), 1935.

Reminiscences of D.H. Lawrence London, (Cape), 1933.

—, Sons of Women. London (Cape), 1931.

Nehls, Edward, D.H. Lawrence: A Composite Biography (3 Vols.) Modison (University Of Wisconsin 1957-59.

Neill, Diana. S. "A Short History of The English Novel", London (1953).

Robson, W.W. "D.H. Lawrence and Women in Love", in The Modern Age. Harmondsworth (Penguin Books) 1961.

Schorer Mark. "Fiction with A Great Burden", in The Kenyon Review, Xiv (Winter 1952) pp. 162-28.

Spilka, Mark. The Love Ethic of D.H. Lawrence Bloomington (Indiana University Press), 1955.

Trilling, Diana. "A Letter of Introduction to Lawrence", in Partison Review, Xxv, I (Winter 1958) pp. 32-48.

Van Ghent, Dorothy, The English Novel: Form and Function. New York (Reinehart), 1953.

Vivas, Eliseo. D.H. Lawrence: The Failure and The Triumph of Art. London (Allen and Unwin) 1961.

West Anthony. D.H. Lawrence, The Novelist Series. London (Arthur Barker) 1957.

Sagar, Keith, The Art of D.H. Lawrence, London: Cambridge University Press 1966.

"Critics on D.H. Lawrence", ed. W.T. Andrews, George Allen and Unwin Ltd. London 1971.

Yudhishtar. Conflict in The Novels of D.H. Lawrence. Ed. A. Noman Jefferes & R.L.C. Lormier. Oliver & Boyd. Edinburg, 1969.

Sinah Omendra, "D.H. Lawrence: Prophet of New Life and Art", National Publishing House. Jaipur, New Delhi, 1997.

Electronic Sources

D.H. Lawrence, Sons and Lovers , http://www.fullbooks.com/Sons-and-Lovers-by-David-Herbert-Lawrence-D.html.

D.H. Lawrence, Women in Love, http://www.online-literature.com/dh_lawrence/women_in_love/.

D.H. Lawrence, The Rainbow, http://www.archive.org/details/rainbow00lawrgoog.

INDEX